If I Just Breathe

by Tina Koral

If I Just Breathe

Published by:
Tina Koral
P.O. Box 394
Glen Ellyn, IL 60138-0394

ISBN: 1440419922
EAN-13: 9781440419928

Library of Congress Control Number: 2008908836

Cover design by Katie Welgat.

Printed in the United States of America by CreateSpace.

For more information, visit www.tinakoral.com

For all those fighting cancer, and for those we have lost.

But most of all,
for Averie

Acknowledgements

This book, and my journey to the other side of breast cancer, would not have been possible without the unfaltering support of my family and friends who have uplifted me in so many ways. Joe, there aren't words that can express how I feel about your endless support and love, in both sickness and in health. I love you always! Special thanks to my mother, Bonnie Blair, who was with me every day of my experience with breast cancer and beyond. I'd also like to thank my brilliant friends and family members who reviewed my manuscript in its early stages and encouraged me to tell this story: Patti Carter, Lisa Castañeda, Karen Geddeis, Gail Pantalena, and Earl Pollack.

Thanks also to the young ladies of the Young Survival Coalition. I'm not sure I could have stayed sane through this experience were it not for your online support. I was no longer alone in this cancer experience after I found you.

Preface

Over 180,000 women are diagnosed with breast cancer every year. Today, there are more than 250,000 women under forty living with breast cancer, and 11,000 more will be diagnosed in the next year. About 1,100 will die from the disease[1].

Young women with breast cancer often have a more aggressive form of cancer than older women. For this reason, early detection and treatment are extremely important to keep the cancer from growing and spreading. Unfortunately, doctors are unaware that young women are at risk for breast cancer, and may misdiagnose their breast lumps as fibrocystic disease, or take a "wait and see" approach, while their breast lumps increase in size and become more difficult to treat.

The misdiagnosis and delayed diagnosis of breast cancer in young women is the most common type of medical malpractice case. The most common allegation in breast malpractice claims is that doctors did not order tests to check for potential breast cancer, and this led to a delay in the diagnosis of cancer, which resulted in injury to the patient

---

1   Young Survival Coalition, www.youngsurvival.org. Accessed 9/15/08.

(the disease progressed to a later and more deadly stage). Typically, the severity of a breast lump is underestimated or mistaken for fibrocystic disease.[2]

Young women with breast cancer deal with a different set of issues than their older counterparts. Women under forty are often building careers and starting marriages and families. Since breast cancer is less common in young women, they often don't know anyone else with the disease in their age group. Isolation is the number one psychosocial issue facing cancer survivors between the ages of fifteen and thirty-nine[3]. When I was diagnosed with invasive breast cancer at the age of thirty, there was a disturbing lack of information about the disease as it affects young women, which increased my sense of isolation. While my friends were getting pregnant, I was getting chemotherapy, and I couldn't find information to help me cope.

If you are a fellow young breast cancer survivor, my hope is that you find comfort within these pages and know that you are not alone. If you are fortunate enough not to have been diagnosed with cancer, I hope that after reading my story you will have the courage to be vigilant in taking control of your own health care decisions, and that you are inspired to be resilient in the face of life's inherent challenges.

Tina Koral

2   Physicians Insurers Association of America Breast Cancer Study, 1999.
3   I'm Too Young For This! Cancer Foundation, www.i2y.org. Accessed 8/30/08

One

In salute e malattia
In ricchezza e povertà
Fino a che morte non ci separi

In sickness and in health
For richer or poorer
Until death do us part

Itightened my grip on Joe's hand as a Roman official read the words that sealed our union as husband and wife. I was both nervous and excited as we stood together, Joe in his tuxedo rented from an eccentric Italian tailor the day before, and me in my strapless white dress with the veil my godmother made by hand. Our marriage took place in a fifteenth century church in Rome in the spring of 2003.

Gabriella, our wedding planner, a Roman native, executed the event with precision. You'd think she even had a hand in planning the weather that day, sunny and warmer than average for April. After the ceremony and some pictures outside the church, we climbed into our rented limousine and headed to scenic tourist favorites, the Trevi Fountain and the Colosseum, for more photographs.

Joe and I were the center of attention as we posed for pictures that day. At the fountain, we smiled as the crowds of tourists politely stepped out of the way of our photos, watching and grinning.

As we smiled for our photographer, Pietro, on a hill outside the Colosseum, a group of about forty school children, all in red caps, repeatedly shouted something at us.

"Do you know what they are saying?" asked Gabriella. We replied that we did not. She said, "They are shouting '*Bacio! Bacio!*' Kiss! Kiss!" Playing it up for our new audience, Joe dipped me backward and planted a long kiss on my lips. The children cheered and Joe pumped his fist in the air triumphantly. Pietro arranged an amazing photo of Joe and I kissing as the children threw their red caps in the air as if in a synchronized display of their excitement for us.

The photographs from that day show a joyful young couple, visibly excited to start a new life together. The promise of a happy home full of children shone in our eyes. The thrill of that day, of marrying my childhood love in a city filled with romance, will stay with me forever. What I did not know at the time was that along with something old, new, borrowed and blue, I carried a seven centimeter, rapidly growing mass of malignant cells in my breast. I was twenty-nine years old.

Ask me where I was when I was diagnosed with cancer. You may as well ask where I was when terrorists slammed airplanes into the World Trade Center. I'll never forget the answers to either question. On the morning of Tuesday, September 11, 2001, I was in my sunny apartment, a fourth floor walk-up in downtown Downers Grove, Illinois, a Chicago suburb. I was just about to leave for the gym, and went to turn off the television that provided background noise while I dressed and ate a quick breakfast. The tone of the newscaster's voice turned more serious, and I moved closer to see what was happening. I covered my open mouth with my hand as I stared at the images of the first tower on fire; I cried when the second plane rammed into the side of the other tower. I thought that would be the one event in my history that I would so clearly remember. My generation's JFK. Unfortunately for me, there would be another.

Monday, August 18, 2003 was the day my personal life was permanently altered, but this time there was no disbelief.

The Friday before, I had undergone diagnostic tests including a mammogram, ultrasound, and finally an ultrasound-guided biopsy of the mass I had first noticed so many months earlier.

I expected to hear the results of the testing on Tuesday, so I planned to just relax on Monday evening after work. Joe was at a White Sox game with a few friends, and while I love having him around, I also enjoy having the house to myself. I had just settled into my favorite chair with a glass of Shiraz and a new John Irving novel I was excited to read. I remember thinking that if the test results were positive for cancer, this may be the last night of my normal life and

I wanted to take some quiet time to settle my mind. I took a few deep breaths and resolved that night, that whatever was to come, I would be strong and fight it with everything I had in me. It must have been the wine talking, because I never felt that confident again.

Just as I finished the glass of wine, the phone's ringing brought me out of the stillness of the moment. When I reached for the phone, the name of my doctor's office displayed on the caller ID.

"Hello?"

"May I speak with Tina, please?" It was Dr. Gee himself. Must be serious, I thought.

"This is Tina." I set my empty wine glass in the kitchen sink.

"Tina, this is Dr. Gee from the breast health center. I've received your biopsy results from Friday, and I'm sorry to say…it is cancer."

Even though I had suspected cancer all along, those words still shook me. Did he really just say what I thought I heard? Here was the confirmation I had been searching for for so long, yet, it brought me no relief. I set the phone down and steadied myself by placing both hands on the kitchen countertop. I took a deep breath. I could hear the tinny sound of my doctor talking in the receiver, and picked it back up.

"Tina, are you there?"

"I'm here. Are you sure it's cancer? My last doctor said it was only a cyst."

"We're sure it's cancer," he said. "In fact, you have four

tumors in your right breast."

"Well, then why would my last doctor say that?" I asked.

"Let's not worry about the past. Come in to my office tomorrow and we'll talk about what kind of cancer you have, and my recommendations for treatment. Is anyone with you tonight?"

"Not right now, but my husband will be home later."

"Are you going to be okay until he gets home?"

"I'll be fine," I lied. What else could I say?

"OK, then we'll see you in the morning."

Damn, I'm in some deep shit. I was numb, and at the same time, knew that those last two minutes were life-changing. I didn't quite know how to react. My first instinct was to scour the internet for treatment options and survival statistics, but I called Joe's cell phone instead. I wanted him with me.

He answered after a few rings with a "Hey baby!" A crowd of Sox fans roared in the background. "You missed a good one tonight! Frank Thomas just hit a two-run homer! They're kickin' Anaheim's ass!"

"I think you need to come home," my voice shaking.

"Why?" he asked, suddenly sober.

"They called with the biopsy results."

"What did they say?" Was he really going to make me say it?

"It's not good."

"Is it cancer?"

"Yes," I yelled. Didn't he get it? Why would I be asking him to come home if it wasn't?

"OK, I should be able to get home in about an hour. Sit tight. I love you."

I placed the phone back on its cradle and went back to my chair. My body went completely limp, while my mind raced with questions. *Now what? What kinds of treatment would I endure? Was I going to die? Why had I wasted so much time in graduate school? Should I cash out my 401k? Why hadn't the other doctors found cancer?*

Those previous doctor visits ran through my head. One with Dr. Kay in February 2002, and another with Dr. Em in November 2003. Both said the mass I had felt was just a cyst and nothing to worry about.

I didn't cry that night. Not even when Joe came home, with an expression on his face that looked like he had just been kicked in the stomach.

"I got here as fast as I could," he said, breathless. He sat next to me on the couch and I fell into his arms. "So what do we do now?"

"We'll see what the doctor says tomorrow, I guess."

"Whatever happens, it'll be fine." I believed him and was able to hold it together that night because I had no idea what was to come. I turned to the Internet for clues to what my future might entail, but learned that treatment options and outcomes vary by the stage and cellular makeup of one's cancer, and I would not know that until my appointment the next day. Joe and I climbed in to bed and settled in for a sleepless night.

Joe and I both took the next day off of work to attend my appointment with Dr. Gee. I remember looking around

15

at the other women in the waiting room of the Breast Center thinking, "You all don't have to worry. I'm the one with cancer." When we met with the doctor, he outlined in detail the results of the biopsy and his recommendations for treatment, which included chemotherapy followed by a mastectomy and radiation. He said that because I had multiple fast-growing tumors, my situation was serious and the outcome could be a complete recovery, or death. It was then that this diagnosis became real to me, and I moved to a state of complete panic. I couldn't believe this was really me, sitting here in this sterile exam room, listening to a doctor tell us that I could die from this. It was like a scene from a sappy Lifetime Television for Women movie.

We also met with a nurse educator who explained my pathology report. I had invasive ductal carcinoma of the breast, the largest tumor measuring seven centimeters, with positive estrogen and progesterone receptors. The nurse discussed in detail the types of cancer cells contained in my tumor, and that they were the rapidly growing kind. When she mentioned that the effects of chemotherapy could leave me unable to get pregnant, I felt any sense of control leave my body. The thought of losing a part of my body was one thing, but losing the chance to create children with the man I loved was heartbreaking. I began to cry hysterically and could not continue the appointment. Once in the car, I immediately went for Joe's cigarettes. Although not a smoker, I smoked the whole drive home. After all, I already had cancer, what difference did it make? I needed to calm my nerves.

Although I knew Joe would be with me every step of the way, I had never felt so alone in my life. My mind went to some very dark places in the days that followed. I couldn't believe that a disease so rare (less than half of one percent of all women diagnosed with breast cancer are younger than thirty) had invaded my body. I was always healthy prior to this, no illnesses, no allergies, not even a broken bone. With no family history of breast cancer, it was just so unlikely that this could ever happen, yet it did. I had no idea what to expect. The only other person I'd known with breast cancer was a childhood friend's mother. It spread to her bones and she died leaving two young children behind.

All I could think was, "I'm going to die," and "I have the worst case of breast cancer ever." I found it hard to get out of bed and cried constantly. Word got out, and friends and family kept calling. I left Joe with the job of explaining what was happening. While I found comfort in every ring of the phone, I didn't want to talk. I knew they would expect me to bravely tell them that everything would be fine, but I didn't believe that, and I didn't feel like acting.

I remember sitting up in bed, looking out the window at Joe with our american bulldog, Molli, and thinking about how I didn't want to leave him; five months of marriage was not enough time. I didn't really have a chance to show him what a great wife I could be. I worried about the extent of the treatment I would need, how my body would look afterward, how others would react to me. Would I be able to work through treatment? Were my days of being healthy over? Would I never get better and just die? I wrote in my

17

journal:

"There is a huge difference between how I am presenting myself to others and how I actually feel. I tell everyone I am doing well, handling it. That's a lie. I'm scared to death and fear the worst case scenario. I don't think my friends and family know how advanced it is."

In the back of my mind I knew I had cancer from the first time I felt the mass. It had taken visits to four different doctors to finally confirm my suspicion. I didn't trust my instincts when I first thought something was wrong. I was made to feel like I was overreacting by three doctors who said my breast mass was just a cyst and allowed it to grow and spread for 18 months. What is the point of doing monthly breast exams, like we are told to do, when no one will listen when you feel a lump? I was angry. I wanted to hold someone accountable. I wanted to prevent this from happening to another young woman. I wanted an explanation. I wanted revenge.

Two

In college, I attended a seminar about the importance of early detection of breast cancer. The speaker passed around a squishy breast model, and we were supposed to close our eyes and feel around to see if we could find the lump. Following that seminar, I regularly performed my monthly self breast exams. When I felt a hard, smooth bump in my right breast near my armpit in December 2001, I thought it would go away with my next menstrual period, which would be normal for a cyst. After two cycles, however, it was still there and did not change shape.

"Joe, feel this."

"Gladly!" he said while reaching for my chest.

"Do you feel that?"

"Right here?" he said as he felt the lump.

"That's it. It's been there for a while."

"Hmm. Well, I'm sure it's nothing to worry about. It's not like it's cancer or anything."

It wasn't the first time I would hear that. I decided to discuss it with my gynecologist at my annual appointment in February 2002 anyway.

It was the first visit to Dr. Kay, an obstetrician and

gynecologist with an office at my local hospital. Until my cancer experience, I'd never had a consistent relationship with a doctor because each time I changed a job, I changed health insurers and physicians. In those years I was finishing a masters degree in public health, and had held a few different jobs and internships over the years.

At the time, I didn't know if the lump was serious or just a harmless cyst, and knowing that early detection was important in case it did turn out to be cancer, I wanted an expert opinion. I arrived at Dr. Kay's office, had a seat in the waiting room, and listened for my name to be called.

After a few minutes, a nurse asked me to follow her into an examination room, and I sat down in a chair next to her. She introduced herself and asked me about my last menstrual period, birth control history - all the usual questions asked at an annual gynecological exam. When she asked me if I was having any problems, I told her I felt a mass in my breast.

"How long has it been there?"

"For almost three months now."

"Is there any pain?"

"No. None."

"We'll have the doctor take a look at it," she said as she scribbled some notes on my chart and handed me a paper gown.

Time passes slowly in a doctor's exam room, and even more slowly when all you are wearing is a paper gown and a pair of ankle socks. After about twenty minutes, I heard the noise of someone removing my chart from the holder outside the door and a quick knock.

"Come in."

"Tina, I'm Dr. Kay," she said as she held out her hand. "It's nice to meet you."

"Thank you, nice to meet you too," I replied.

Dr. Kay quickly looked over my records, and then began a routine pelvic exam. Finding nothing unusual, she began to gather the chart and said I should come back in a year for my next check up.

"Dr. Kay, I was hoping you'd be able to feel this lump in my breast. I'm not sure if it's anything serious, but it has been there for a few months and I'd like your opinion." Dr. Kay put my chart back on the desk and asked me to lie back. She made small, circular movements while pressing down on my breast. I pointed out the area where I had felt the lump.

"This here?" she said as she felt the exact area.

"Yes, that's it."

"That doesn't feel like anything to be concerned about. It's really common for women your age to have what are called fibrocystic conditions. It's just a fluid-filled cyst. It will probably go away in a few months."

"So, it's nothing then?" I asked.

"It's nothing. We'll see you back in about a year for your next exam." I thanked her and began to dress, relieved that I had nothing to worry about.

In the months that followed, Joe and I were engaged and shortly after bought a house in Glen Ellyn, a suburb about twenty-five miles west of Chicago. I had continued with my monthly breast self-exams, and the mass persisted. About eight months following my appointment with Dr. Kay, the lump was still present and a new symptom emerged. One morning, I woke up with what looked like two drips of something yellow on my pajamas right over my right nipple. The first time I noticed the stain, I thought it was from something I had eaten or drank the night before. But when I saw it again the next morning on a clean t-shirt I had worn to bed, I wondered if it had come from my breast. I lifted my shirt and squeezed the nipple with my thumb and forefinger. Sure enough, out came a drop of yellowish fluid. I began researching breast conditions on the internet and found that this was not normal.

I'd read that most often the cause of nipple discharge is pregnancy, lactation, or a hormonal imbalance. Normally, however, these conditions will cause discharge from *both* breasts. It is considered abnormal if the discharge is only on one side, and could signal a breast infection, mastitis, or breast cancer. I knew it was time to get a second opinion.

Since we had moved, and Dr. Kay's office was no longer convenient, I scheduled an appointment with a doctor at a large teaching hospital near Chicago. I wanted the expertise that I assumed was inherent in an institution of this hospital's size and reputation. I was also eager to start a relationship with the doctor I imagined would one day deliver my babies.

I was a little nervous as I arrived at the hospital for my appointment in late October, 2002. After the research I had done I knew there was a problem, but thought it could be corrected in a minor surgical procedure or perhaps with medication. After entering the examination room I told the nurse about the mass, how long it had been there, and described the discharge. I also explained that in the last day or two I noticed that when I bent over, say to turn on the water in the bathtub, my nipple became inverted. She jotted this down and left me to wait for the doctor.

Dr. Em is an imposing figure, standing over six feet tall. He had grey hair, and looked to be in his early sixties. He introduced himself without even looking up from my chart, and asked me the standard questions you might expect at a gynecological exam. He conducted the pelvic exam and moved to my breasts.

"Is this the lump?" he asked as he palpated the spot.

"Yes, that's it.

"How long has it been there?"

"About eleven months."

"It feels like a cyst. They're very common in women your age. Any family history of breast cancer?"

"No. No one in my family has had any kind of cancer that I know of."

"Well, because of your age, and family history, I'd say you have nothing to worry about." Dr. Em said as he sat down to make a notation in my chart.

"But I'm also having discharge from that same breast. Should I be concerned about that?" I pressed as I sat up from the table.

"That's called galactorrhea. Breast milk. All women have that," he said without looking up. I felt like I was hitting a brick wall with him. I didn't think it was possible for a woman to produce breast milk unless she was pregnant, and I had never been pregnant.

"Isn't there a test I can have to make sure?" I had been living with this lump for almost a year, and now this discharge was, well, just gross. I wanted it resolved. A leaking breast is not very sexy after all, especially for a newlywed.

"If it will make you feel better, I will write an order for a mammogram," he said, somewhat annoyed. "But women your age have dense breasts, so mammograms usually can't detect anything."

"Okay," I said, hoping that despite his pessimism, the mammogram would help us determine exactly what the problem was.

Dr. Em wrote an order for the mammogram and handed it to me, instructing me to make an appointment with the secretary before I left. Once outside the exam room, I read the order form on which Dr. Em had written, "asymptomatic with no palpable lump." I found that to be strange, especially since it seemed like Dr. Em clearly felt the mass and I told him about the discharge. Weren't those symptoms?

When I returned to the hospital four days later for the mammogram, Joe came with me. I was starting to get nervous about the whole situation, and wanted some moral support. I clutched Joe's hand as we entered the building with the sign in front that read, "Cancer Center."

I signed in at the breast imaging area with my name and date of birth and handed the order to the nurse at the front desk. I turned to take a seat in the waiting area, but was stopped short.

"This is an order for a screening mammogram. We don't do screening mammograms on women under thirty years old," she said.

"I'll be thirty in eight months."

"Sorry, we can't do it until you are thirty. We'd be causing more cancer than we would find if we started mammograms that early."

"But my doctor ordered this because I have a breast lump."

"You need to go back to him and ask for a *diagnostic* mammogram. Your order says that you have no symptoms." Annoyed, I took the order back and we went home.

The next business day, I called Dr. Em's office. The call went directly to his office voice mail. I left a message that morning, and another in the afternoon when I didn't receive a return call. I was finally able to reach a nurse in Dr. Em's office the following day. She said Dr. Em was unavailable, so I relayed the story about the denied mammogram to his nurse. She told me she would talk to him and call me back. When she did, the next morning, she asked if she could fax me an order for an ultrasound.

"Why is the order for an ultrasound and not a mammogram?" I asked.

"Because an ultrasound can tell us if a lump is solid or cystic."

"I'm sure that's helpful, but Dr. Em originally ordered a mammogram. Why did the order change?"

"I don't know, I guess he changed his mind. What's the

fax number, I'll send it now."

I was confused by this. I didn't understand why Dr. Em would originally order a mammogram, then switch to an ultrasound when I requested a diagnostic mammogram. Repeated messages left at his office went unreturned. I decided to get the ultrasound, trusting that Dr. Em had a reason for this change.

The following week, at the ultrasound visit, I was asked to remove the clothing above my waist and put on a hospital gown. The ultrasound technician led me into a darkened room and asked me to lay on my back on a cushioned table. She asked me to point out where I felt the mass and squirted a cold gel onto the spot. Pressing the imaging tool into the spot I indicated, she slid it back and forth while looking at a monitor displaying black and white images.

I had seen ultrasounds performed on pregnant women on television, and have seen a few ultrasound pictures of developing fetuses, but I have never had an ultrasound conducted on me. I watched the screen showing the grey and black images of the inside of my breast, and could not make heads or tails of it. I knew black means "fluid," and white means "tissue," but could not identify where the mass was on the screen. After capturing some images, the technician called for the radiologist, who took a quick look and made for a hasty exit.

"Excuse me," I said politely as she headed for the door, "Did you see anything abnormal?"

"No, all I saw was a cyst. All women get them."

"So, is there treatment for this, or what happens next?"

"Your doctor will contact you if he wants to do further testing, but I did not see anything."

I contacted Dr. Em's office three times but had no success in obtaining the official ultrasound report.

Much later, I learned that the radiologist's report noted dilated milk ducts, but indicated that they were "fluid filled structures indicative of a fibrocystic condition."

I was relieved. It wasn't cancer. I knew this because three doctors now had told me so. I could put the fears that I now thought were unreasonable behind me. I was left in a state of comfortable ignorance while the cancer was left to grow unchallenged for nine more months.

Three

The months of my life following the ultrasound were extremely full. I was planning our overseas wedding, which mandated a daunting amount of paperwork for the Italian Embassy here in Chicago and the American Embassy in Rome. All of the frustration, however, paid off when I finally married my childhood sweetheart in the wedding of my dreams.

"Joey" Koral was the first boy I ever had a crush on. While I don't remember the first time I laid eyes on his cute blond hair and blue eyes, I do remember that we were paired up by our kindergarten teacher, Mrs. Grass, for a performance of the "Bunny Hop," where kids stand in a line, holding on to the waist of the person in front of them. They tap the floor with their right foot, then with their left foot, then they hop forwards, backwards, and finally three hops forward to finish the sequence, which continues throughout the song. I don't remember if he was holding my waist or if I was holding his, but that was the event that sparked the romance, at least on my end. My crush continued for years until I was heartbroken in the seventh grade when his father's job was transferred to Arizona and the family followed. But young hearts are resilient, and I went on to fall in love with other blond-haired, blue-eyed boys. Joe and his family eventually moved back to the Chicago area during our high school years, and we ended up having the same group of friends. Although we never dated in high school or for years after, my first boyfriend, a friend of Joe's, would tell me that Joe would always warn him, "Be good to Tina or I'll steal her away from you!"

Joe and I lost touch for a couple years following college, and both of us dated other people, but none of them were "marriage material" for either of us. In 1999, internet dating was hot and I would sometimes browse online personal ads. I didn't think I would ever actually meet anyone with an ad, but it was fun to look at the pictures and read their descriptions of the perfect mate. I had never seen an ad for anyone I knew until Joe's picture popped up. I was shocked to see that he had an ad and I was pleasantly surprised to see he was still as good looking as ever. I immediately e-mailed him.

Apparently, Joe and his best friend and coworker Mike had a contest going to see how many responses they could each get from their personal ads. Neither of them had any intention of contacting anyone who responded. Whenever a woman would e-mail to express interest, Joe or Mike would yell, "Got one!" and continue to read the message aloud. But when Joe saw my e-mail, he yelled, "Oh, shit!" and he immediately deleted his ad out of embarrassment that someone who knew him had seen it.

Lucky for me, however, he did reply to my e-mail and we met up at a nearby jazz club a few weeks later. A couple of weeks and a few more dates after that, we made it official that we would date exclusively. I knew immediately that the timing was right, and that from then on we would always be together. I think he had a feeling too; on our second date he mused aloud, "Maybe we're soulmates." Two years later, he proposed to me on the playground of our grade school.

From November 2002 when I'd had the ultrasound, until June of 2003, the mass in my breast continued to grow. Before this, it was a small, smooth, pea-shaped lump. After a few months it changed into a thickness that filled half of my right breast. Based on what the doctors had told me, I thought that this was nothing more than maybe a group of cysts developing around the original one. I decided to see a new physician because I was unhappy with the care I had received from Dr. Em. I remembered how he made me feel like I was overreacting when he downplayed my symptoms, and how difficult it was to get test results from his office. I made an appointment with Dr. Jay at her office two blocks from my home.

 I noticed the look of concern on her face as she started the breast exam and felt the large area, and my heart sank. She commented that it did not feel normal, and recommended further testing. She referred me to a breast surgeon, where I had a mammogram, ultrasound, and finally a biopsy, on Friday, August 15, 2003. I was diagnosed the following Monday.

Early on, I was told that I had Stage 2 breast cancer, which is defined as a cancer that either involves axillary (armpit) lymph nodes and is less than five centimeters, or is over five centimeters and does not involve any lymph nodes. One of my lesions was estimated to be seven centimeters, and my doctors did not feel anything in my armpit, which is how they arrived at the Stage 2 diagnosis. After chemotherapy and my mastectomy, however, twenty-four lymph nodes were removed, and one had a small amount of cancerous cells present. This put me at Stage 3A – a mass over five centimeters with lymph node involvement. The American Cancer Society estimated my chances of surviving five years to be 56%.

This was a difficult piece of information to swallow, to say the least. My chances of making it to thirty-five years old were only 50-50? All of the years of study and work that I had put into my career now seemed like a waste of time. I wouldn't even have my student loans paid off by age thirty-five! Would I live long enough to have children? Would I see them grow up? It was incredibly scary to think the time I had left could be so short.

I had an extremely negative frame of mind in those first few weeks. I was horribly depressed and afraid of what was to come. I thought about how small my chances were of even getting breast cancer at the age of thirty (one in 2,500) and expected the worst. I'd also read that women who are diagnosed at a young age usually have a more aggressive cancer and die from the disease more often. I recoiled from family and friends; not wanting to have to explain, once again, what was going on. They wanted to know why I got cancer. What the treatment was going to entail. If I planned to quit my job. They were questions I couldn't answer and didn't want to think about.

I was angry. I had placed my confidence, blindly perhaps, in three doctors who told me that the mass was a common cyst. I was angry at them for not performing the tests necessary for a proper diagnosis, and angry at myself for not trusting my instincts and insisting on proper care.

Since Dr. Gee recommends a second opinion to all his patients, I returned to the hospital where I had seen Dr. Em. Even though I'd had such a poor experience with him, my research showed that the oncology department of this institution was the best in my area. I met with an oncologist, radiation oncologist, and breast surgeon, and four days after my diagnosis a treatment plan was developed.

Due to the size of the tumor, a lumpectomy (surgical removal of just the mass and a little surrounding tissue) was out of the question. My right breast would need to be removed completely. While I had always thought my breasts were my best physical feature, I didn't think twice about letting them go. I wanted to get rid of the cancer by whatever means necessary. I knew that with reconstructive surgery my chest could look normal again one day, and with clothes on, no one would know the difference. I asked Joe how he felt about me losing a breast. He told me I was much more than just two breasts and that he is more of a "butt man" anyway. It was the first time we laughed since the diagnosis.

Neoadjuvant chemotherapy (chemical treatment before surgery) was recommended to shrink the tumor to help ensure a better chance of getting the whole tumor out during surgery. I would be given Adriamycin and Taxotere, a cocktail administered to women with locally advanced breast cancer. Commonly, this blend is given in tandem with a third drug, Cytoxan, a drug that is particularly damaging to the ovaries. Since my dream was to start a family, I asked not to receive it to help preserve my chances of getting pregnant later. My oncologist agreed to forego Cytoxan until we could see how my tumor reacted to Adriamycin and Taxotere. If there was no shrinkage, she would add it back to my regimen. I was scheduled to receive chemotherapy on Mondays, and my supervisor at the medical association where I worked graciously allowed me to take the rest of the week off work to recover. I would then work for two weeks, and this pattern would repeat for five cycles.

I had mixed emotions the day I went for my first round of chemotherapy. I was scared to death, envisioning a hospital room filled with bald, vomiting cancer patients. At the same time, I was ready to start fighting this uninvited beast. The chemotherapy room turned out to be a lot different than I expected. Yes, everyone there looked to be as old as my grandparents, but overall they weren't as scary looking as I imagined despite the collection of wigs, scarves, and baseball caps. After having my temperature and blood pressure taken, a nurse explained what each drug was, and what the side effects would be. The Taxotere came in a clear intravenous bag that dripped into a needle stuck into a vein in my wrist. It was a harmless looking colorless liquid. Adriamycin, however, is a bright red liquid, the color of cherry Kool-Aid, that is pushed into the IV with a big syringe. Adriamycin is affectionately called "the red devil" by those who have had the pleasure of receiving it. If it is dripped onto the skin by accident, it will cause necrosis, or death of the skin tissue. The nurse wore two gloves on each hand while pushing it through the syringe. I was told to flush the toilet twice following treatment so that there would be no chance of a family member coming in contact with my urine, which had turned red from the powerful drug. Despite all of these precautions, they were injecting this stuff into my body?

The chemotherapy drugs are cold. I shivered at every drop that entered my arm through the IV, and envisioned it traveling through my bloodstream up my arm to my right breast. I felt empowered. I was fighting back. Killing what was trying to kill me.

Joe and I were in need of a new bed, and the week before chemotherapy started we bought a new one. It had two air mattresses inside, allowing Joe and I to choose how soft or firm we wanted our side to be. This is where I spent most of my time during treatment, on my super-soft side of the bed, Molli nuzzled up under my arm. I had never felt so strange, so *sick*. I felt like I did when I was sent home sick from school as a kid, like I just wanted to be taken care of. I wanted my mom to bring me a plain hamburger from McDonald's, served up with ginger ale, like she did years ago. When I mentioned this to Joe, he brought me a hamburger from McDonald's, but this time it tasted like sand. Everything tasted different, which is why it's common cancer knowledge never to eat any of your favorite foods after chemotherapy, because they won't be your favorites for long. I still have not been able to bring myself to eat a McDonald's hamburger.

Unfortunately, in addition to cancer cells, chemotherapy drugs also kill some good stuff in the process, particularly other fast growing cells like hair cells, causing the characteristic hair loss. It also kills cells in the stomach lining causing nausea, vomiting, diarrhea, and loss of appetite (although some marijuana provided by a friend helped with that, giving me the "munchies"). A terrible metallic taste in my mouth could only be masked by Doritos. Fatigue and nausea had me down for about three days following each treatment. I had become a tired, pot-smoking, junk-food eating, bald cancer patient, but the worse I felt, I rationalized, the better the weapon was working.

I was lonely. I didn't know anyone with cancer, and I never saw anyone at the cancer center who was anywhere near my age. After Joe left for work each morning, I'd be left alone with my fears of how this would all turn out. I take that back, I was not totally alone. Molli snuggled closer each time she heard me cry.

It was during the early days of chemotherapy that I came across The Young Survival Coalition website and bulletin board. When I started browsing the messages on the board, I read about other young women who were writing about the same issues I was facing. They had concerns about their careers, their fertility, and their marriages and relationships, all as they related to cancer. I had finally found a home. I spent hours each day communicating with other young women with breast cancer, and day by day, the fog of loneliness and isolation lifted. I began to let my friends and family in on what I was experiencing. My frame of mind started to turn to the positive and the fighter in me emerged.

Four

Ihung my head over the bathroom sink and gently raked my fingers through my hair from the nape of my neck to my forehead. Pieces of hair fell into the bowl as silent as snow.

"It's coming out," I called to Joe, who was watching a baseball game in the living room.

"No it's not."

"It is. Come look." He came into the bathroom and saw a mound of light brown hair in the sink bowl. He inspected my head and stuck his finger onto a bald spot the size of a quarter above my right ear. His finger was cold and strange on my bare scalp.

Just the week before, I had a mass of long, curly hair, enough for two women. I've always disliked the unruly curls that never looked good, no matter what length or color. My hair just always looked messy, not elegant and sleek like the straight hair of the models that fill fashion magazines. Many times while trying unsuccessfully to get my hair to do what I wanted it to do, I'd think in frustration, "One day I'm going to shave it all off," not knowing that one day I actually would.

My doctor said it would be more traumatic to lose long hair and recommended I get a short haircut. She said it would start falling out about fourteen days after the first round of chemotherapy. It may sound strange, but at that time I was excited for it to begin falling out. It meant the poison was working. I was also curious to see how I would look without hair; how I would feel. Would I have a nicely shaped head? Was some strange Mikhail Gorbechev-like birthmark hidden beneath my hair?

"Honey, I need help. I want to shave it tonight." We had talked about this before my first chemotherapy treatment - that I would get a short cut, then shave the rest of my hair off when it started coming out on its own. Not only was the falling hair a mess on my pillow and in the shower, but taking it off myself was one way I could take some control of the situation.

Joe plugged the clippers into the power outlet and turned them on. The initial sound was startling, and as he moved them closer to my head, I moved away.

"I can't do this," he said, and turned the clippers off, setting them on the bathroom sink.

"Joe, you have to help me. I won't be able to do the back of my head by myself." With trepidation, he retrieved the clippers and turned them back on. I closed my eyes and hung my head back over the sink.

When he was finished, I looked up to see a different person in the mirror looking back at me. He had shaved it without a guard; all that was left was stubble. My head was surprisingly nice and round, and I did not have any birthmarks or forgotten-about scars. My scalp was white where it had previously been covered with hair. My eyes looked big with dark circles underneath. Now I looked like a cancer patient. I cried as I made a loose ball out of the pile of hair left in the sink. The tears blurred my vision so that the hair looked like some small, furry animal.

I had read about a woman who took the hair she had shaved off and placed it on her driveway. She watched from a window inside the house as birds flew away with pieces of it. She imagined her hair being used in nests, to make shelter for new life. Looking back, I wish I had done something like that, something ceremonial. Instead, I placed the ball of hair in my bathroom wastebasket and went to bed.

I awoke to a new fear: making it to the office without hair. People in this situation might dread facing their co-workers, but I was more afraid of the hundreds of stares I knew were waiting for me from the many strangers I would encounter during a typical commute.

I lived in the suburbs of Chicago, but my job was in the city. I lived within walking distance of the train station and, once aboard, it was about a 40-minute ride to Chicago. From there, I could walk to my office if the weather was nice. If not, I would take a crowded city bus.

"Good luck, honey," Joe said and pulled me close for a goodbye kiss. I pushed my hat, carefully chosen to coordinate with my outfit, onto my head and headed for the train station. I used the half-mile walk to build up my courage, thinking *I can do this*, and *maybe they won't even notice I am bald*. I took deep breaths as I approached the station and the crowd of over 100 commuters lined up along the tracks.

I've often compared walking down the train station platform to where the front cars stop, where I preferred to sit, to walking a fashion runway. People stand along the sidewalk parallel to the train tracks as commuters in their smart business wear walk confidently toward the area that correspond to their preferred train car. I walked past the mass of people, trying to mask the terror I was feeling inside by holding my head high and staring straight ahead. I wondered if people noticed my overnight transformation.

A few days prior I bought a wig, thinking I would wear it every day to conceal my bald head. With the help of two sweet older women who were "used to this sort of thing," I chose a wig that had straight, light brown hair. I thought it was a nice, neutral look, nothing too extreme. It looked realistic and even had subtle highlights. I took it to my stylist who trimmed it so that it would look a little more natural. We giggled when another customer at the salon complemented me on my highlights. The morning after I had shaved my head, I tried the wig on, and just couldn't go through with wearing it in public. I felt like an imposter, like I was in some kind of disguise, trying to be someone else.

I decided to wear hats instead. Because it was chilly outside I thought I would easily slip by unnoticed, but I could tell immediately that people still noticed something was missing. Once on the train, I promptly buried my head in a book, but when I looked up, I saw people glancing my way. At first I thought I was just paranoid, imagining what I thought were curious looks, but the way they would quickly look away when our eyes met told me the truth. After I lost my eyebrows and eyelashes it became even more difficult to hide the fact that I was undergoing cancer treatments. One of the worst things about having cancer and undergoing chemotherapy is not the hair loss itself, but that once it is gone you can't hide your illness from anyone. You can walk past a group of people with any number of embarrassing or traumatic events in their lives; maybe one is an alcoholic, maybe another just lost their job. Another may be going through a divorce or the death of a loved one. But you can't tell just by looking at them. With cancer, any stranger on the street can look at you and know what is going on medically whether you want them to or not. I felt so raw and exposed, and angry that I didn't have the option of privacy.

I made it through that first commute without hair by blocking out my thoughts with music, my ipod drowning out the nervous chatter in my head. I played one song in particular, *Breathe* by Michelle Branch over and over that day, and loud.

> *If I just breathe*
> *Let it fill the space between*
> *Everything is all right*
> *Breathe – every little piece of me, you'll see*
> *Everything is all right*
> *If I just breathe*

This song reminded me to do just what it said – breathe, everything is all right. When I saw the stares – *breathe*. When a strong gust of wind almost blew my hat off – *breathe*. When I thought about how drastically my life had changed in such a short space of time – *just breathe, everything is all right*. These healing breaths allowed me to center myself, push back the tears, and focus on getting through the day.

I sometimes joked to others about the benefits of hair loss, like being able to sleep twenty minutes longer in the morning because I didn't have to wash, blow dry, or style my hair, or not having to shave my legs. But the hair loss was truly one of the most painful parts of my whole cancer experience.

Navigating the world without hair is a lesson in humility. Any confidence I had pre-chemotherapy was gone. During the six months of baldness, I declined social invitations and even passed on an all-expenses paid cruise that Joe's parents offered us. I was tired of being the only person around wearing a hat – indoors. It was difficult to discover that so much of my self-esteem was wrapped up in my appearance.

I learned I was not alone. While sitting in the waiting room of my oncologist's office, I read an article about the effect of hair on self-esteem and learned that bad hair, or at least the *thought* of bad hair, leads to lower self-esteem. People feel less smart, less capable, more embarrassed and more self-conscious. Since I did not have the luxury of staying home during my cancer treatments, these were feelings I dealt with every day. I remember turning down a speaking engagement at work because I just couldn't imagine being taken seriously looking as I did.

Luckily, when chemotherapy is over the hair always grows back, and I was no exception. I constantly rubbed my head to check for growth, and about six weeks after my last treatment, I reached up to feel stubble on my previously smooth dome. Family and friends commented that it was coming back quickly, but to me the regrowth was painfully slow when all I wanted was to feel normal again. I took B-complex vitamins twice daily because I had read they stimulated hair growth (I'll never know if this really worked). When my hair was about an inch long, I ditched the hats, colored it blonde, and hoped people would think I was extremely cool and hip, not a recovering cancer patient.

Now, my hair looks much like it did before cancer. It is still curly and unruly, and I have more grey than before, but I'm happy to have it. No one who looks at me today would suspect I had a cancer experience in my past, and I am grateful to be able to keep that part of my life from strangers or others who I wish not to tell.

Hair is a symbol of youth and an expression of beauty and personal style. While losing it was one of the worst parts of my cancer experiences, it was a blessing in disguise because I learned a lot about myself, the way I look at myself, and the way I look at other people who are going through difficult times. I felt the kindness of my friends and family, who threw a "Hat Party" for me; each attendee brought me a hat as a gift and wore a hat themselves. I felt the love of my husband, who rubbed my bald head every night while we watched television. I felt the camaraderie of a community of cancer patients who gave me knowing smiles in the cancer center waiting room, my bald head a membership card to a club I eventually became proud to be part of.

Five

I began considering the possibility of initiating a lawsuit against Dr. Kay and Dr. Em soon after I started chemotherapy. At first, my thoughts about suing them revolved around some type of revenge for the delay I experienced. The thoughts of revenge quickly subsided as reality took over, but I knew I still had to take some kind of action. I sued because I truly believe that had I been older and presented with the exact same symptoms, they would have sent me for additional testing. If I was over forty, I believe my mass would not have been dismissed as just a dilated duct and Dr. Em would not have convinced me that the discharge was galactorrhea. In a sense, I experienced a form of age discrimination and prejudice. I don't expect perfection from my health care providers. I do expect the care that is standard for the symptoms I present with.

I wanted to make Dr. Kay, Dr. Em, and both of their institutions think twice the next time a young patient presents with similar symptoms. The only option, for me, was to sue. The settlement I expected to receive could never be used to buy my breasts back or to purchase the years of life that may be lost as a result of my advanced stage of cancer, but it would help ensure financial stability. It would be there should I need it for expensive fertility treatments that might be necessary if I can't conceive children due to the damage that chemotherapy can cause. It could be used to pay for medical treatments should I have a recurrence, which was more likely due to progression of the disease that I experienced because of the delay in diagnosis.

I had reservations about initiating a lawsuit at that point in my treatment. I was concerned that I would not be able to handle the additional stress the case might bring, and that it would be too emotionally draining. All of my concerns were dismissed after meeting with my lawyer one Saturday morning in October. The meeting was the week of my second of five chemotherapy treatments, and I was bald and tired. Joe came with me for support and we met Andrew, a medical malpractice attorney who was recommended by my next-door neighbor and lived just a few blocks away.

Andrew was in his late forties, with a friendly smile and a welcoming demeanor. However, as the three of us and his old beagle climbed the stairs behind his house to a loft-office above the garage, I wondered just what I was getting myself into. *Is this guy a real lawyer?* I thought. Andrew must have read the question on my face and assured us that while he loved to work in his home office, he did actually work for a large legal firm with a real office in downtown Chicago.

"Tell me why you're here to see me," Andrew said once Joe and I sat down across from his desk. When I was finished, he immediately said he would take the case, that it sounded strong, and that it appeared that both Dr. Kay and Dr. Em were negligent in the way that they handled my care. He thought that both doctors and their institutions should be sued, but that the case was much stronger against Dr. Em because I'd had more contact with him and he had more opportunities to do the right thing and didn't.

Andrew explained that the delayed diagnosis of breast cancer is the most common type of medical malpractice lawsuit. It's an alarming set of events, but not unique. A young woman discovers a mass in her breast and becomes concerned. She decides to discuss it with her OB/GYN doctor. Her doctor feels the mass, but tells her not to worry about it, that she does not fit the profile for cancer. She is under forty years old, and has no family history of breast cancer. Her doctor tells her it is a cyst and to wait and see if it goes away in a few months. The woman is later found to not only have breast cancer, but to have metastatic breast cancer due to the delay in diagnosis.

Many young women go undiagnosed while their cancers continue to grow inside them because their doctors think they are simply too young to get breast cancer, or doctors choose to roll the dice and not order necessary diagnostic tests in an effort to reduce costs.

Based on his experience, Andrew said the case would be wrapped up in two to three years and would most likely settle out of court. I signed the contract which allowed Andrew to pursue the case, and turned my focus to staying well during treatment.

Soon after my diagnosis I wrote Dr. Em a letter,

never intending to send it. I merely wanted to organize my feelings about his role in my illness.

Dear Dr. Em,

I am sure you were surprised when you found out you were named in a medical malpractice lawsuit this week. I'm sure that when we met you never expected this to happen. That's because you didn't suspect I had cancer. I'm sure you know from your extensive medical background in women's health that breast cancer is rare, but still possible in young women. You knew that, yet you chose to play the odds with my life by not ordering the necessary tests that could've diagnosed me much sooner.

How many young women have you examined before or since my visit that complained of breast lumps? Did you tell them that they were too young for cancer too? Or that they don't have to worry because they have no family history? Do you remember saying that to me? You were wrong.

About one in 250 women under thirty get breast cancer. How many other patients of your's might have a cancerous tumor growing in their bodies as you read this? Did you know that cancer in young women is usually more aggressive? Did you know it is usually diagnosed in later stages and that leads to poorer outcomes? Your poor medical care directly contributed to the advancement of my cancer.

Why didn't you just aspirate the mass to be sure it was a cyst, as you said it was? It would've taken just a few minutes. And why didn't you order a diagnostic mammogram? Why didn't you take me seriously? Why did my symptoms fail to "impress" you?

I hope that as a result of this you learn that what you did, or failed to do, was wrong. Because the delay of my diagnosis caused my tumor to grow to seven centimeters and spread to my lymph nodes, I may never make it to my 40th birthday. I might never have babies or see them grow up. Worst of all, I might have to leave my husband before I am ready.

You're a teacher. Learn from this and teach your students to follow every breast mass until a proper diagnosis can be made. Don't let what happened to me happen to your next young patient who comes to you for guidance, concerned about a breast lump.

During my time off following chemotherapy treatments, I had lots of time to research breast cancer. The first thing I do when faced with something new, good or bad, is research it on the Internet or in the library. I hit the medical library at the hospital where I was being treated.

I mentioned before that Dr. Em was a teacher of medical students. After some online snooping, I was able to find the list of textbooks that Dr. Em requires his students to read, and began to review them myself. I was surprised at the many differences in Dr. Em's care compared to the recommendations outlined in the textbooks that he himself taught from.

When I discussed the breast mass with Dr. Em, he performed a breast exam and told me that he felt it. He stated that because of my age and lack of family history of breast cancer, that this mass was a cyst, which is common. He did not recommend a biopsy or any follow up (I later asked for the mammogram). In my medical record, he noted, "no gross mass is palpable," even though he said he felt it in the exact area where I had. *Danforth's Obstetrics and Gynecology,* one of the textbooks Dr. Em recommends to his students states, "Once a mass is identified, a diagnosis must be assigned and cancer ruled out," and "The accepted standard of care is to excise all solid, three-dimensional masses unless a definite benign diagnosis can be made by FNA [fine needle aspiration]," and, "There is no lesion that is obviously benign." *Current Obstetrics and Gynecologic Diagnosis and Treatment,* edited by Martin L. Pernell, sums up my case perfectly when it states, "…about 15% of lesions believed to be benign are found to be malignant. These findings demonstrate the fallibility of clinical judgment and the necessity for biopsy." Obviously Dr. Em thought he was infallible. Did he think he could tell if a lump was malignant or benign just by feeling it through layers of skin and breast tissue? Or did he just not care enough and decided to take a chance that it was benign?

I was able to find information about breast discharge in these texts as well. The Pernell text states, "Unilateral, spontaneous serous or serosanguineous discharge from a single duct is usually caused by an intraductal papilloma, or rarely, by intraductal cancer. In either case, a mass may or may not be present," and, "Cytologic examination of the discharge should be accomplished and may identify malignant cells." So, whether or not Dr. Em palpated the mass in my breast, he did see the discharge from one side, and could have sent a sample away for diagnostics, and might have discovered the cancer that way. Danforth's states, "All significant nipple discharges warrant referral for tissue biopsy," and, "If the drainage first appeared in the patient's bra or nightgown on awakening, this finding is more significant than discharge during a workout at the gym." All this time my body was trying to tell me that it was cancer, and no one would listen. Not even me.

At my request, Dr. Em referred me for a screening mammogram. When I arrived, I was refused because of my age, and was told that giving screening mammograms to women under the age of thirty would cause more cancer than they would detect due to the exposure to radiation. *Comprehensive Gynecology* by Droegemuller, et. al. counters that with, "…the risk of radiation from mammography is negligible compared with the benefits of the discovery of early and potentially curable breast carcinoma."

Later, Dr. Em referred me for an ultrasound, even though the Droegemuller text states, "…ultrasound should not be used as a sole imaging technique for breast disease."

Finding all of these instances where the medical text differed from Dr. Em's care reaffirmed my decision to take legal action. I know that my cancer could have been treated at an earlier stage and my chances of survival could have been greater if Dr. Em had followed the guidelines outlined in these texts – the texts he relies upon to train future doctors. I shared my research with Andrew, hoping it would be useful in my case.

Six

My fifth and last chemotherapy treatment was December 1, 2003. By Christmastime, I had some soft, blonde fuzz on my head, but no real growth. I had read that it would take three months from the last chemotherapy treatment before my hair would start to grow back, and I couldn't wait. After all, I had been completely bald for about three full months already, and Chicago's winter winds can be cold on a hairless head!

Thankfully, I experienced a complete pathological response with chemotherapy, meaning there were no signs of cancer on the scans that were taken after my five treatments. However, because of the aggressiveness of my cancer, a mastectomy was still the recommended course of action. Sometimes the cancer cells are still there, but are too small to be seen on the scans. I didn't want to take a chance of this killer returning.

My right breast was removed on December 16, 2003. I opted for immediate reconstruction so I would never have to experience being flat. I'll never forget the feeling of dread as I waited in the pre-op area at the hospital with Joe, knowing that any minute I would be taken away to have my breast amputated. I was terrified of the anesthesia, and my fears were heightened when I was told it was time to give my glasses to Joe and say goodbye (I am legally blind without corrective lenses). Joe was a rock as he gave me a kiss and said everything was going to be fine, while I erupted in tears.

The trans-rectus abdominis muscle (TRAM) flap reconstruction took nine hours and required a blood transfusion due to a large loss of blood during the surgery. My old breast was replaced with a mound of flesh comprised of abdominal tissue, muscle, and skin taken from my abdomen. Before the surgery, I had a little blue butterfly tattoo just under my belly button, *a la* Drew Barrymore. After the surgery, it had migrated to my new breast, which always gave my oncologist a chuckle. My plastic surgeon said this could be removed during a future surgery.

I woke from surgery, and in my groggy state repeatedly asked Joe to get my glasses, which were in his car. While I don't remember any of this, he said he was trying to talk to me to assess how I was feeling and I just kept saying, "Can you get my glasses?" It might sound trivial, but it was scary to wake up from surgery, sleepy and unable to see, when all I wanted was to be awake and alert.

I can honestly say that I have never looked worse than I did after that surgery. In addition to being wrapped in bandages and surgical tape from my chest to my lower abdomen, I was bald, wearing my glasses (which I rarely wore in public because the lenses are so thick) and didn't have any makeup. Imagine my terror when one of my nurses ended up being an old friend from junior high school that

I had not seen since then. *She* looked beautiful. *I* was at my lowest of lows.

After five days in the hospital I was sent home for six weeks of recovery. Because I had tissue and skin removed from my abdomen, I could not stand up straight or lay down flat for over a month. If I tried to, my skin would pull on the stitches causing unimaginable agony. My mom called to tell me that everything would be fine, that I'd start feeling better each day. I knew she was right, but it was hard to believe when I couldn't get out of bed unassisted. I couldn't move my right arm. I couldn't sneeze or cough or laugh without searing pain.

Before I'd even had a chance to recover from the mastectomy, I started a set of thirty-three external beam radiation treatments. They started out easy enough, a couple of minutes under the radiation machine, five days a week. It actually takes longer to get undressed than for the actual treatment. As much as I tried to relax, I shook each time I slid under the accelerator machine. I meditated, repeating my mantra over and over: "All will be well. I will be well," with each breath in and out. I used this mantra many times during the course of treatment, while having bone scans, awaiting surgery, anytime I needed to calm down and gain control.

At first, radiation seemed to have no effect. I maintained my energy level and did not have any burns. But the effects of radiation are cumulative, and I was soon extremely fatigued and experienced severe burns on my new breast. Radiation caused a section of the transplanted skin on my breast to turn black and deteriorate, which took months to heal. The burns, however, did not cause any pain because the whole area was numb from the mastectomy and reconstruction.

I was always the youngest patient in the radiation waiting room, but that was nothing new. And I was always dressed up for work, while the other patients were dressed casually and comfortably. After treatment, Joe was always waiting for me, ready to take me to the nearby train station that I took into the city. I would strut down the radiation center hallway, grab my husband's arm, and walk out of there like I was going to resume my wonderful life. That's the image I wanted to portray, if not to convince anyone but myself.

About half way through my radiation treatments, I started to feel more confident with my new look. I ditched the hats and braved the world with my crew-cut. I received lots of compliments on my new 'do at the cancer center, but in the real world, my look was received with stares.

Then, treatment was essentially over. No more scans, and no more treatments, besides a daily tamoxifen pill. I tried to put the whole experience behind me, but that proved to be difficult.

About six months following my last radiation treatment, I realized I still had not moved on. Joe attended a friend's bachelor party which included the customary trip to a strip club. Now, my husband is not one to visit this type of establishment regularly and has only been to strip clubs in the company of fellow bachelor party attendees, so I don't have a problem with it and was never threatened by his going. He's not the type that would be interested in a lap dance, so I know it is just harmless "observation."

When he came home, I peppered him with questions. How was the party? Did the groom have fun? How many people came? Did you get a lap dance?

"Nah, why would I want a lap dance when I have you at home?" he said.

"Yeah, why would you want that when you have these?" and I kind of pushed up my breasts and shook them a little. Then I realized, why wouldn't he want to see big healthy breasts? How will he ever be happy with mine, one much smaller than the other, streaked with angry, red scars and without a nipple? Could it really even be called a breast? I started to cry and went into my bedroom.

Joe followed me and sat down next to me on the bed. He explained that my breasts are not what makes me and that he would love me no matter how I looked, if I had two breasts or no breasts, or two heads. It just wasn't important to him. But I realized how much healing I still had to do if I was to move beyond cancer. I made an appointment to visit a counseling psychologist the next day. Therapy became an instrumental part of my healing process.

Seven

The house of my youth was one of seven 1960's split levels that formed a ring around Willow Court, which served as the location of much of my childhood play. The concrete circle was our kickball field, bike track, and where we played Kick the Can and Ghosts in the Graveyard. The court was usually devoid of cars, which made it a safe place to play. If a car drove in, most of the time it was one of the residents of the houses lining the court and we respectfully ceased play to let them pass. If the car was unrecognizable, someone using the court as a turnaround perhaps, we would ignore it, barely moving aside to let it by, and usually flashing an annoyed look at the driver.

The time after dinner when we were allowed back outside to play, and before the streetlights came on when we were expected to return home, was when the court would come alive. Sixteen children would spill out of those seven homes equipped with bigwheels, wiffle ball bats, cardboard boxes that served as bases, hula hoops, and other paraphernalia of childhood.

My house was one of the prettiest on the court. My family kept it in meticulous shape, from the evergreen bushes in the front landscaped area that were cut in the shape of a spiral, to the area under the pine tree that was always raked free of pine needles. We had a large, round, above ground pool in the backyard and a huge vegetable garden where no weed could hide. The grass was always perfectly manicured and the house itself always looked clean and fresh.

From the outside, life on Willow Court was idyllic, the perfect Chicago childhood. None of my neighbors knew what a frightening, chaotic, and disturbing place the inside of our home actually was.

I never saw my father drink anything other than beer after 10 a.m. He had a glass of milk with breakfast, but after that, his only source of fluids was Pabst Blue Ribbon. He drank it constantly. In the garage, while watching TV, even while driving. The liquor store where he bought his beer sold plastic covers that one could slip around a beer can to make it look like the beer was a can of pop, only, instead of Coca-Cola, it read, Caco-Calo, written in the same white script over the same red background as the more popular drink. My father had a Caco-Calo, a 7OP, and a Pipsi cover stashed in the glovebox of his old Pontiac Bonneville to disguise his driving drink of choice.

All of this drinking had an affect on his health. He always seemed to have a stomach ulcer, and I was routinely awakened at five o'clock a.m. by the sound of his vomiting in the one upstairs bathroom.

A culture of dysfunction characterized my family. My father, drunk and abusive, was unable to fulfill the typical fatherly roles. While he was able to hold a job and worked for the same plumbing company for over 20 years, allowing my mother to stay home with my older brother, my younger sister and me, he was not the least bit caring, loving, or attentive. His ability to support us financially eventually turned into a trap. My mother never went to college after getting married and pregnant at nineteen, and stopped working her secretary job just before my older brother was born. Years down the road, when things became really unbearable for her, she did not have the skills necessary to land a job, make her own money, and get us all out of this mess.

Home life was unpredictable and inconsistent. I would never dream of bringing friends over after school because I never knew what was going on inside the house when I got home. My father could be in a drunken rage about some minor infraction committed by my mother, usually having to do with the state of his dinner or something just as trivial. This could lead to something as benign as a hole punched in a wall or as indescribable as my mother getting pummeled in the face, rendering her unable to be seen in public without wearing her big sunglasses. While my mother was usually his preferred punching bag, my older brother was also routinely beaten, mostly as a result of reports of behavioral issues at school which were almost certainly caused by the beatings at home. It was the definition of a vicious cycle.

While I do remember him hitting me, I know that my mother and brother absorbed much of the physical abuse. My father seemed to enjoy hurting me in more emotional ways, knowing that I was a very introspective, sensitive kid. In my seventh grade history class we were studying the Great Depression and were assigned partners to build a diorama of a shanty town, which sprung up in America in the 1930's due to the wide scale spread of unemployment. My partner was a girl named Jenny, who was also a friend of mine. I went over to her house a few days after school to build our shanty town, which we believed would be the best in the class. We spent hours putting together the miniature shacks made of corrugated cardboard and scrap plastic, complete with tiny shirts and pants hung out "to dry" on a yarn clothesline, with miniature trees scattered about.

I brought the model to my house the night before the project was due to complete some final touches. That evening, my father was like a tornado of rage moving through the house fueled by many cans of beer and anger over the fact that the lawn had not been mowed before he'd arrived home from work. When he made it to my bedroom, he looked at our project, said, "What's this piece of shit?" and brought down his fist with enough force to smash the houses and crack the piece of plywood they were mounted on. The little trees went flying all over my bedroom. He left my room and moved on to his next target without even acknowledging I was there. I remember the anxiety mounting as I tried to take in what had just happened, and realizing I would have to come up with some kind of excuse not only for why I was not able to turn in my assignment, but why Jenny should not be penalized for not having one either. Obviously, I couldn't tell my history teacher the truth, so I said I dropped it while carrying it to the car that morning and didn't have time to fix it before school. It was just one of the many lies that we told to cover up the embarrassment of my father's actions. We learned early on to keep the family's secrets. "Don't tell anyone about what goes on in this house," became the family motto. My mother told me that if anyone found out what was going on, I woul be put in a foster home. At times I though that might be a better option than living at home, but I did not want to leave my mom.

Confusion and fear marked most of my childhood. I always felt different from other children because I had this big secret to hide. I never had the opportunity to just be a kid, like the other kids in the court and my friends at school. I was always very much concerned about what was going on at home and how I could keep everyone else from finding out. I was never completely comfortable playing with other children because my concerns about the problems at home clouded everything.

In the middle of the night, when my father came home from the bar and eventually woke us all up with his yelling, I'd lie awake and posit different lives for myself. I'd go from being the daughter of my soccer coach to a runaway living on the streets of Chicago, from a girl orphaned when her parents were killed in a plane crash to the daughter of a wealthy businessman. Any family where the father wasn't drunk and abusive would do. Imagining a new life somewhere else helped me fall back asleep, only to awake in the same hell.

Even today I can still hear my brother's screams as my father whipped him with a belt, and my mother's crying. After hearing it so many times over the course of my most formative years of life, it's ingrained in me and still painful to recall.

Throughout my life I've heard so much about how divorce devastates children, and how difficult it can be on a family. It was just the opposite for me. I prayed for my parents to divorce. I couldn't understand why my mom didn't just leave my dad. Later I learned it was because she thought he was going to die as a result of his drinking, either in an accident on the jobsite or while driving his car. If he was dead, she wouldn't have to deal with what she was sure would be a difficult divorce, and we would all be free from his abuse. But that never happened and I guess she tired of waiting. When I was sixteen my mother arranged for me to stay at a friend's house while she and my sister went to a secret shelter for battered women. My father was forcibly removed from our house by the police and all the locks were changed. I never saw my father again. I expected life to be better without all the craziness he brought us, but it took some time to adjust. I was angry at my mom for staying with him so long and not getting us out of harm before then. That, and the normal disagreements between mothers and teenagers, led to me moving out a couple of years later. I didn't speak to my mom for about three years.

My mom and I have a great relationship now, over twenty years later, and talk easily about our former lives. But it's almost like we're talking about some other mother and daughter. Once we were talking about the things we tried to do as a family to have fun every once in a while, like play board games, swim in our pool, or play miniature golf.

But having fun was just never fun. The spontaneity within us was squashed by fear. She said, "It was really hard to get into it and really have fun, because you never knew when someone was about to get punched," and we laughed hysterically. Maybe we laughed out of relief in knowing that our lives would never be like that again, and maybe it was to cover up the sadness that we both feel for all of those wasted years.

Besides Joe, I was able to lean on my mom while I was sick. She's a very strong lady, despite being a petite five foot one. She is soft spoken, warm, and approachable. She's often told how young she looks for her age because she is so cute. You'd never guess by looking at her today that she suffered nearly twenty years of cruelty at the hands of my father. After he left, she built her life back on her own, working a secretarial job while running a craft business. After a while, she met a truly nice man and retired with him in Florida. When I was able to take a week off work following each chemotherapy treatment, my mom called me every day around lunchtime. I unloaded all of my worries about cancer, not being able to have children, and the possibility of death. And she just absorbed it all.

Considering that I never learned how healthy families related to each other, I am sometimes surprised that Joe and I have such a strong relationship. Typically, adult children of alcoholics become alcoholics themselves, or marry one. Thankfully, I am an exception to the rule. And this is no coincidence. I made a conscious choice long ago not to let my destructive father destroy the rest of my life.

I survived my childhood by escaping, not physically, but in my mind via books and writing. I was always in the middle of a book, experiencing the wonders of Narnia, exploring Terabithia or chasing butterflies in the Secret Garden. So while in a counseling session the psychologist asked if I could apply my survival method of the past, escape through books, to my current situation, I realized that I couldn't escape cancer. It was inside my body and I couldn't run from it. I had to fight it and use all my power and everything medicine could provide to kill it. I know that if I could survive my childhood, then I could, I would, survive cancer too.

While there have been no definitive studies linking stress to cancer, I have to believe it was a contributing factor in my case. I was diagnosed at age thirty, and it is often said that breast cancer can grow for ten years before getting big enough to be detected. My first sixteen years where filled with fear, anxiety, anger, and sadness, which I beleive impacted me not only psychologically, but physically. Of course, this is just a theory, because in the absence of any family history of breast cancer, I will never know why it happened at such a young age.

Eight

My love of gardening has strengthened each year since owning my own yard, to the point where one year, on a night late in February, I was unable to sleep because in my mind I walked step by step through my garden, visualizing my perennials poking up through the soil.

Perennials are garden plants that return year after year. Unlike annuals, which die when the weather turns cold, perennials simply wither down to the roots, disappearing into the soil. The roots, however, remain alive, ready to push new stems and leaves into the spring sunlight. The regrowth of perennial plants comes from the stem and roots.

My cancer experience mirrors the lifecycle of the perennial. The period of my life preceding my diagnosis was a time when I was growing, learning how to function in a marriage four months old and already full of sunny days and rarely a rainy one, excited to take on a colorful phase of life. I was taking root in my new role as a wife and looking forward to blossoming into a mother.

When the diagnosis hit, it was like being stepped on, crushed. I made treatment decisions in a daze, all of the unique or colorful aspects of myself withering away until my old personality was gone.

I was in hibernation for eight months, from September 2003 until April 2004. I wasn't myself. I was an actor trying to fool people into thinking I was the old me. I was going through the motions of treatments, work, and everyday life behaving like nothing had changed, when in fact, everything about me had.

Our 1926 bungalow is situated toward the front of a long, narrow lot. The back twenty-five feet was overgrown with weeds that had become trees. The good thing about these tree-weeds is that they are easy to remove, having a very shallow root system that required just a few plunges of a shovel to unearth.

Ever since we bought the house, I had wanted to clear out this area and plant a shade garden under the tall oaks and maples. The spring following my mastectomy I became obsessive about clearing out the brush and weeds. I commanded Joe's help, and on one particular Saturday we worked tirelessly, with only a short break for lunch. In late afternoon Joe dropped his shovel, proclaimed that he was done for the day, and turned toward the house. I remember getting upset because I wanted to keep going until the area was clear so we could rototil it the next day. He asked me why I was so adamant about finishing the job, since we had all summer to work on it. I didn't have an answer until a couple minutes later when the realization hit me, *That's what this is all about. I'm preparing a place to die.* Overwhelmed with sadness, I became conscious that I had been working so hard at beautifying the yard so that I would have a pretty place to spend my last days. When Joe saw my tears, I explained them away by telling him my arm was aching, and we went inside the house to relax.

Realistically, I had no reason to think I would succumb to cancer. Odds are, if any cancer cells lingered following a mastectomy and chemotherapy, they would have been killed by the radiation treatments I'd received. But I couldn't let go of the fear that I still had cancer somewhere in my body that just hadn't been detected yet.

Summer rolled around and I slowly came back to life; exercise, counseling, and anti-anxiety medication were my fertilizers. We evenutally cleared out the back area and planted my shade garden. I began the process of moving beyond cancer. I learned so much about myself during this time, most importantly that the depth of my strength is not apparent to others, in fact to most people I appear to be overly sensitive. My husband just knows to expect tears at every sad movie or wedding. Before this experience I would not even have considered myself a strong person. But like the perennial plant, my power is ingrained deep within me, in my roots, in my very being. Difficult experiences in my earlier years have prepared me for my battle with cancer, so that I would be able to not only live after I had beaten it, but also to thrive.

I was, and am still, very afraid of dying. A huge part of my fear is leaving Joe, not having enough time together. But perhaps the time Joe and I have together will never be enough; I will always want to be with him. If we both live to be ninety years old, I'll still be afraid to leave him.

It's not the actual act of dying that I am afraid of, nor do I have any regret for things I haven't done. I've done a lot in my thirty-something years on Earth. I've survived the chaos of growing up with an alcoholic father. I've won first place in a flute contest. I lost and re-established my relationship with my mother. I've paid my way through college and earned a master's degree. I've had my own apartment. I've floated above the Arizona desert in a hot air balloon. I've traveled through Europe. I've loved deeply and became the wife of a wonderful man. I've left former employers better off than they were before I was hired. I've ridden a bike down a volcano in Hawaii. I've owned a house and maintained a garden that fed my family. And I've survived cancer. But despite everything I've done, I still wanted more from my life. I wanted to be a mom.

Nine

My dreams of motherhood needed to be put on hold until after I finished a course of hormonal therapy with tamoxifen. Tamoxifen is prescribed for hormone positive cancers, and because I had such advanced disease taking it would further reduce any risk of recurrence. The standard course of treatment is five years. Pregnancy should be avoided while taking the drug to avoid the risk of birth defects. Before cancer, Joe and I had planned to get pregnant in fall of 2003, when I was thirty. Now I had a decision to make. Don't take tamoxifen and get pregnant - while taking the chance that the thousand-times increase in estrogen caused by pregnancy would fuel a recurrence, or, take tamoxifen for five years – prolonging the heartbreak I already felt because we didn't have kids and increasing the chance of infertility or complications because by then I would be thirty-six years old.

I compromised. I asked my doctor about the possibility of stopping the drug after two years in order to try to get pregnant. She explained that while being on it for five years held the maximum benefit, there was still some benefit to be gained in the first two years. She knew how important having a child was to me because we talked about it soon after I was diagnosed when treatment plans were being made. At that time, I refused one of the three standard chemotherapy drugs because of its toxic effect on the ovaries. With my doctor's approval, I decided to stay on tamoxifen for two years, stop the drug and get pregnant as soon as possible, then resume the treatment.

I continued working and pursuing my legal case against Dr. Em and Dr. Kay. Andrew told me that two expert witnesses, both breast surgeons, had been located and had reviewed my case. The expert witnesses determined that both doctors had not followed the standard of care when they failed to figure out just what the mass in my breast was. The opinion of these expert witnesses further strengthened my case and it continued to move forward.

In late June I received word from Andrew that he and the defense lawyers wished to schedule my deposition. July 12, 2005, the day after my 32nd birthday, was the day I was to give my side of the story. Andrew said it was probable that Dr. Em would be in the room while I was deposed, as it was his right to do so. While this made me nervous, Andrew assured me that if I simply told the truth, everything would be fine. He said not to let Dr. Em intimidate me, be clear and concise in my statements, and to admit that I could not recall an event or conversation if I really was not sure of specifics.

Joe took the day off of work to lend some moral support; he knew I was terribly nervous. We met Andrew in the lobby of an office building in downtown Chicago, then headed up a few floors to the meeting room. When we walked in, Dr. Em, his lawyer, Dr. Kay's lawyer, and a court reporter were already there. I did not make eye contact with Dr. Em, and tried to pretend he was not even in the room. I was sworn in, and Dr. Em's lawyer, a thin, well-dressed woman in her fifties, began the deposition by asking my full name.

A: Tina Theresa Sophia Koral.

Q: Thank you. Ms. Koral, my name is Margaret and I represent Dr. Em and the hospital in this matter. I'm going to be asking you questions pursuant to the rules. And I need to tell you a few ground rules, which your attorney has probably gone over, so I will be very brief. The court reporter has to take down everything I say and everything that you say, so we can't talk at the same time. The other thing is that you need to answer questions with words and not sounds like "uh-huh" and not gestures of your hands or shaking your head. Okay?

A: Okay.

Q: And the other rule is that when I ask you a question I'm going to assume that in answering it, my question was clear to you. If however, my question is not clear to you, please tell me what is unclear so that I can try to correct it. Is that clear to you now?

A: Yes.

Margaret began by asking me some warm-up questions

about Joe, where he worked, how long we were married, my address, and who lived with me. She asked my sibling's names and ages, and if there were any family members or friends who had any information about the issues in the case. I stated that my mother did, because she called me each day from Florida and knew exactly what was going on from my angle. I was asked about my educational background, and current and past employment. Then she drove to the heart of the matter.

Q: At some point you noticed a mass in your right breast, is that correct?

A: Yes.

Q: When was that?

A: It was approximately December 2001.

Q: And tell me how you came about noticing it?

A: During regular monthly breast exams I noticed that there was a mass in the nine o'clock area of my right breast.

Q: Describe for me how you performed your regular monthly breast exams.

A: Well, I would lift the arm of the breast I was doing the examination on and make circles starting from the inside and going toward the outside of the breast.

Q: When you did your monthly breast exams, were you standing, sitting, or lying down?

A: Usually lying down.

Q: So was December of 2001 the first time you found any irregularity in either breast?

A: Yes.

Q: Describe for me what you felt.

A: I found a hard, round lump that felt smooth and was moveable.

Q: And what do you mean by "moveable"?

A: That it didn't feel like it was attached to my chest or the skin at the surface of my breast. It felt as if it were floating in the tissue between the two.

Q: In December of 2001, did anyone else feel what you felt?

A: Yes, my husband did.

Q: And he at the same time could also feel it?

A: He said he could.

Q: And what medical person did you tell about this discovery in December 2001?

A: I didn't tell any medical person about it in December 2001.

73

Q: When was the first time that you told any medical person about what you noticed in December 2001?

A: In February 2002 when I met with Dr. Kay.

Q: So between December 2001 and February 2002, did you do anything to address the mass you had felt in September?

A: Yes, I made an appointment to see Dr. Kay.

Q: What was the purpose of you going to see Dr. Kay in February 2002?

A: I had not had an OB/GYN visit in a couple of years, so I was going to establish care with her, discuss birth control, and ask about the mass I felt in my breast.

Q: So the three reasons in your mind for seeing Dr. Kay were to establish OB/GYN care, explore birth control options, and examine the mass?

A: Correct.

Q: Did you have to call and make an appointment with her?

A: Yes.

Q: And when you called and make the appointment, did you indicate those three reasons – establishing gyne care, birth control, and the mass as the reasons you wanted to see her?

A: I don't remember.

Q: When you got to the office, who did you see?

A: Once I was in the examining room?

Q: No, when you walked in the door of the address of the doctor's office.

A: I don't remember.

Q: Did you speak with a nurse?

A: Inside the examining room? Yes.

Q: Did you tell anyone before you actually were in the examining room about the lump in your breast?

A: No.

Part of me wanted to ask – who would I tell about the mass before I was in the examining room? The receptionist? People in the waiting room? Standard procedure for a legal deposition, I'm sure, but I was not accustomed to this. I put my growing frustration and annoyance aside and remained calm.

Q: When you were in the examining room, who did you tell about the mass in your breast?

A: First, I told the nurse.

Q: Okay, and what did you tell her?

A: That I had a mass in my breast. *We were going around in circles now!*

Q: Were you specific that it was your right breast?

A: Yes.

Q: And did you tell her like you testified that it was in the nine o'clock area?

A: I don't remember.

Q: Did you tell her what it felt like as you testified when you described it to her?

A: I don't remember.

Q: So, when Dr. Kay then began her examination, were you completely undressed and in a robe?

A: Yes.

Q: And did Dr. Kay examine your breasts?

A: Yes.

Q: Did she do an exam of your entire body?

A: She did a pelvic exam and a breast exam.

Q: Describe the breast exam for me.

A: I was lying down on the examining table, and she

placed her hands on my breasts and when I pointed out where I felt the lump, she acknowledged that she felt it too.

Q: What did Dr. Kay say about the lump?

A: She said it felt like a cyst.

Q: And did Dr. Kay, when she was doing the exam, in your opinion, was she in the same area of the right breast that you had felt the lump?

A: Yes.

Q: So there wasn't any question in your mind that she was feeling the same thing that you felt?

A: No, there was no question.

Q: Did she describe what she meant when she said it felt like a cyst?

A: No.

Q: Now, what did Dr. Kay suggest you do?

A: I do not recall there being any plan for follow up. I don't recall any suggestions, other than to return in a year for the next exam.

Q: Other than what you've described that you had felt in December 2001 and then what you indicated Dr. Kay said she felt in February 2002, did your right breast have any physical characteristics or look different than it had in the past?

A: I did notice more superficial veins on the right side when compared to the left, but I don't recall when I started to notice that.

Q: So you don't know if you noticed any physical appearance different in the right breast in December 2001?

A: No, I don't recall.

Q: And you don't know if you noticed the superficial veins looking different in February 2002?

A: Correct, I don't know.

Q: What you're telling me is that at some point in your diagnosis you did notice a difference physically in how the right breast looked as compared to the left?

A: Correct.

Q: Did you notice any discharge in December 2001?

A: No.

Q: Did you feel anything different in the right breast in December 2001?

A: Other than the lump, no.

Q: I meant, was it painful?

A: No.

Q: In February 2002 did you notice any discharge?

A: No.

Q: And in February 2002 was there any pain associated with the lump?

A: No.

Q: When you were in the examining room with Dr. Kay, did she put your hand on what she felt to indicate it was the same?

A: No.

Q: You testified that you didn't believe there was any follow up planned. Did Dr. Kay tell you to come back into her office in three months?

A: No, I believe she asked me to return in a year for my regular OBGYN exam.

Q: When you left Dr. Kay's office, what was your understanding of what you had in your right breast?

A: That it was a cyst.

Q: Was the word "cyst" actually used by Dr. Kay?

A: Yes.

Q: Did Dr. Kay indicate to you that there was any testing that could be done to confirm it was a cyst?

A: She did not indicate that, no.

Q: Did Dr. Kay instruct you to continue your monthly self-examinations?

A: I don't recall.

Q: Did you continue your monthly self-examinations?

A: Yes.

At this point, Margaret began asking me if I continued to see Dr. Kay following this appointment, which I did not. Her office was located near the apartment where I lived at the time, and when Joe and I purchased a house in another town, I decided to see another doctor. This turned out to be Dr. Em.

Q: When is the first time that you saw Dr. Em?

A: October of 2002.

Q: Now, between February of 2002 with Dr. Kay, and the October 2002 appointment with Dr. Em, did you do monthly breast exams?

A: Yes.

Q: Did each of your monthly breast exams have the same result that it did in September of 2001?

A: The mass had remained about the same size, but in

August 2002, I believe, I began to notice a discharge from the right nipple.

Q: Describe that for me.

A: I would notice a yellow discharge on the inside of my bra and on my nightclothes. It happened every day, and every night.

Q: Were you aware of it while it was happening?

A: No.

Q: So you just saw the discharge itself?

A: Correct.

Q: And who did you tell about the discharge that you noticed in August of 2002?

A: My husband and my mother.

Q: Did you seek any medical exam or advice with regard to the discharge in August 2002?

A: I made an appointment with Dr. Em, but I don't recall how long the wait was between when I scheduled the appointment and October 3, 2002, when I actually had the appointment.

Q: And when you called, did you specify you were interested in seeing Dr. Em?

A: No, I stated I was interested in seeing an OB/GYN doctor, and I guess they assigned me to him.

Q: And did they ask you to gather any records with regard to previous care?

A: No.

Q: Tell me about the appointment with Dr. Em. Did you have a conversation with him regarding why you made the appointment?

A: I believe so.

Q: And what were those reasons?

A: Again, to establish OB/GYN care, and to get the mass looked at.

Q: Did you have any other complaints that you told Dr. Em about?

A: Prior to the appointment with Dr. Em, I considered participating in a clinical trial of a new method of birth control that was being conducted in a medical office in the same building where I was working. I'd had a physical exam there, where they told me I had an enlarged thyroid. So, I wanted to ask Dr. Em about that as well.

Q: Was the breast abnormality that you found in September 2001 of concern to you?

A: Yes, very much so.

Q: But it was not enough of a concern that you mentioned it when you called to make your appointment with Dr. Em?

A: I did not feel it was necessary to discuss it with the receptionist that scheduled the appointment. *Was she kidding?*

Q: How did your breasts look at that time?

A: At some point following the appointment with Dr. Kay and prior to the appointment with Dr. Em, I also noticed a puckering of my right nipple.

Q: During your conversation with Dr. Em, prior to him examining you, what did you tell him you were worried about or any symptoms that you had?

A: I told him about the breast mass and asked about the enlarged thyroid.

Q: Was the enlarged thyroid your main concern during your examination and discussion with Dr. Em?

A: No.

Q: What was your main concern?

A: The breast mass.

Q: And what did you tell Dr. Em specifically about the

breast mass?

A: That I had felt one, and that I was experiencing discharge out of that side and had noticed the slightly puckered or inverted nipple.

Q: Did Dr. Em do a pelvic exam?

A: Yes.

Q: What were you wearing at the time?

A: A cloth gown.

Q: Did he do a breast exam?

A: Yes.

Q: And describe how Dr. Em did the exam.

A: I don't recall specifics, but I was lying down, and during the exam I told him where the mass was located and he acknowledged that he also felt it.

Q: Did Dr. Em ask you to bend over so that he could see the inversion of the nipple as you described?

A: No.

Q: When you were sitting up, was the inversion of the nipple present?

A: No, just when I bent over.

Q: Did Dr. Em make any comments to you about his findings on the breast exam?

A: Yes. He said that it felt like a cyst. I explained that I had discharge and he said it was galactorrhea, breast milk, and that it was normal. He was able to express the discharge by squeezing the nipple. I recall him asking about a family history of breast cancer, and I said there was none.

Q: So part of the exam involved squeezing the nipple?

A: Yes.

Q: And you indicated earlier that Dr. Em said he felt something like a cyst. Do you remember that testimony?

A: Yes. He said he had felt the mass in my breast where I indicated that it was, and that it felt like a cyst to him.

Q: So it was your understanding that you and Dr. Em were both talking about the same area of the right breast?

A: That was my understanding, yes.

Q: Up until this point, has any medical professional described your breasts as dense?

A: I don't believe so.

Q: Has any medical professional described your breasts as fibrocystic?

A: No.

Q: When you do your breast exams, other than the mass, do some areas of your breasts feel thicker than others?

A: I never noticed anything that felt abnormal other than the mass.

Q: Would you say that the consistency of both of your breasts at that time felt the same?

A: Yes.

Q: Back to more details about Dr. Em's exam. At what point did he say that he thought it felt like a cyst? Was this after all of the physical exams?

A: Yes.

Q: And did Dr. Em tell you that you needed to do anything?

A: No, he did not.

Q: Didn't he tell you that you needed to follow up with an endocrinologist with regard to the thyroid?

A: I asked for an appointment with an endocrinologist. I don't recall Dr. Em suggesting that I see one.

Q: Did Dr. Em indicate to you that you needed to get a mammogram?

A: He did not indicate that I needed one, but I requested one.

Q: Okay, so regardless of whose idea it was, you left the

appointment with a plan to see an endocrinologist and a plan to have a mammogram, correct?

Margaret was clearly annoyed, but I wanted to make it clear that Dr. Em did not suggest any follow up, I had to ask for it.

A: Correct.

Q: So, you indicated that Dr. Em didn't tell you to get a mammogram, but somehow you got an order for a mammogram that was from Dr. Em?

A: Correct, I asked Dr. Em for the order.

Q: Why did you ask for a mammogram?

A: Because I was concerned about the mass and the discharge and I really felt that further testing was needed. Even if it was just a cyst, I wanted it treated. I didn't want to wake up each morning with discharge on my clothes.

Q: And when was your appointment for the mammogram?

A: A few weeks later.

Q: Did Dr. Em ask you to return to him at any particular time?

A: I don't believe so.

Q: Did Dr. Em tell you to make another appointment if you notice any changes?

A: No.

Q: Did anyone at the clinic indicate to you that you needed to make a follow-up appointment?

A: No.

Q: Did Dr. Em ask you to return in three months?

A: No.

Q: Obviously you didn't make an appointment for three months later.

A: No.

Q: Did you have a mammogram?

A: I did not.

Q: Why not?

A: When I went to the appointment, the nurse on duty said that the order was for a screening mammogram, and since I was under the age of thirty they would not do a screening mammogram on me. She said they would cause more cancer then they treat if they gave mammograms at such an early age. She said that the order should have stated that I needed a diagnostic mammogram.

Q: Then what did you do?

A: I called Dr. Em's office again, left several messages,

and finally told them what had happened with the mammogram, and asked what I should do next. I was then told to make an appointment for an ultrasound, which I did.

Q: When was the ultrasound performed?

A: In early November.

Q: Did you have any discussions with the radiologist or technician during the ultrasound?

A: Yes. I told them my symptoms – the mass, the discharge and the inversion of the nipple, and the location.

Q: Did the radiologist make any comments to you?

A: Yes, she said the mass looked like a cyst, and that they were very common. She told me to contact Dr. Em for the full ultrasound report in a few days.

Q: Did you do that?

A: I phoned twice and left messages but was not able to get the results and did not follow up after that.

Q: Did you ever receive an understanding of what the ultrasound showed other than what the radiologist said and before your diagnosis?

A: No.

Q: You didn't follow up?

A: I did not, no.

Q: Was your main concern at the time your thyroid?

A: No.

Q: But you followed up on the thyroid but not the ultrasound?

A: Well, by that time I've had three different doctors tell me that it was a cyst, so no, I did not follow up.

Q: Who were the three doctors that told you it was a cyst?

A: Dr. Kay, Dr. Em, and the radiologist.

Q: Did the discharge ever change?

A: No.

Q: After you were given the thyroid medication, did it change?

A: No.

Q: Did the discharge remain consistent from the time you discovered it through your diagnosis?

A: Yes.

Q: When was your breast cancer eventually diagnosed?

A: It was diagnosed on August 18, 2003.

Q: Prior to that date, you went to see another OB/GYN doctor, is that correct?

A: Yes.

Q: Why did you not return to Dr. Em?

A: Because I was not satisfied with the care I received from Dr. Em.

Q: Why were you not satisfied?

A: Because he was very condescending to me during the appointment. He basically blew off my symptoms and did not take them seriously. It was also difficult to get any responses from his office.

I looked over at Dr. Em, who was looking at me incredulously with raised eyebrows and his head tilted to the side.

Q: You say that you were unsatisfied with Dr. Em's care because he was condescending. Please explain that.

A: To me, it is condescending when a doctor does not take your complaints seriously. He failured to recommend further tests. I had to ask for additional tests. He indicated that because of my age and lack of family history of breast cancer that the mass was just a cyst. I left feeling like I was overreacting about the situation.

Dr. Em was shaking his head and writing something on

his notepad.

Q: Between the time of the ultrasound in November 2002 and the next time you saw the new OB/GYN in July 2003, was there any change in the breast?

A: Yes, the mass was much larger.

Q: Why did you go to see the new OB/GYN?

A: I had become extremely concerned about the mass.

Q: What about the discharge, did that change at all?

A: No.

Q: And was the inversion of the nipple the same as well?

A: Yes. The superficial veins were there at that time as well.

Q: What did you tell the new OB/GYN with regard to your symptoms?

A: I told her about the mass and the symptoms I spoke of earlier - the inversion of the nipple, the discharge and the veins - and how long I had experienced them.

Q: And did the new OB/GYN do a breast exam?

A: Yes.

Q: And what did she say to you with regard to the results of this exam?

A: She said she was very concerned, and referred me to a breast health center for further testing.

Q: And when did you go to the breast health center?

A: My appointment was Friday, August 15, 2003.

Q: And what happened at this appointment?

A: Well, it started out with a manual breast exam by the physician, who appeared to be concerned with what he felt. I ended up having a mammogram, an ultrasound, and a biopsy that day.

Q: And when did you learn the results of these tests?

A: The following Monday, August 18, 2003.

Q: What were the results?

A: I had multiple areas of cancer in the right breast.

Q: What was your next step?

A: To return to the breast health center the next day to discuss treatment options. I went the next morning. We discussed their proposed treatment plan, and they recommended I get a second opinion, which they suggest for all patients.

Q: Did you get a second opinion?

A: Yes. In September of 2003 I met with another oncology

team, and their conclusion was that I was not a candidate for a lumpectomy and that I should have a mastectomy following chemotherapy. So I would have chemotherapy first to shrink the tumor because it was so large at that point.

Q: And when was chemotherapy planned to begin?

A: Immediately. I believe I started the week after I was diagnosed.

Q: Can you describe your chemotherapy regimen?

A: I had Adriamycin and Taxotere together every three weeks.

Q: After chemotherapy was completed, I think that was in December 2003, what was the next part of your treatment?

A: I had a right mastectomy and lymph node dissection on December 16, 2003.

Q: What were the results of the lymph node dissection?

A: I had one cancerous lymph node out of the 24 removed.

Q: Was a breast reconstruction done?

A: Yes, immediately following the mastectomy.

Q: After the chemotherapy, mastectomy, reconstruction, and your recovery period, did you have any problems?

A: Well, after the surgery I had thirty-three sessions of

radiation.

Q: Okay, then tell me how you felt and what your reaction to any of those were. We can break it down by treatment I guess if that is easier for the record. Let's start with the chemotherapy.

A: I felt horrible.

Q: Tell me how.

At this point I began to get emotional. All of the pain and fear I felt during treatment came flooding back. This, paired with the stress I was feeling while discussing the case in a room filled with lawyers and Dr. Em, was too much to handle. My eyes welled with tears.

Q: We can take a break at any time.

A: I'm fine. During chemotherapy I was nauseous and very tired. I would take a week off work following each chemotherapy treatment, then work the following two weeks. This cycle continued for five treatments, about four months. I lost my hair, and it was very difficult to continue a normal life without any hair.

Q: And when you would go back to work, would these symptoms subside?

A: Well, obviously not the hair loss. I felt tired at work, and still nauseous at times, but to a lesser degree compared to the week following treatment. I also just felt insecure because of my appearance at work. I felt like people were staring at me. Once in a crowded elevator, when I was wearing a hat, a co-worker said to me, "So, did you lose all your hair yet?" I was mortified.

Q: Let's talk about the mastectomy. Can you tell me the effect the mastectomy had on you?

A: Well, the surgery itself was painful, as well as the six weeks of recovery from the reconstruction procedure. I could not stand up straight or sleep flat for about four weeks. I had a loss of the range of motion in my right arm due to the lymph node dissection, which still continues and limits certain activities. The scarring is psychologically difficult to deal with, as is the loss of sensation in the breast and armpit area.

Q: Is the reconstruction surgery complete?

A: No, I have another surgery next week to finish the reconstruction.

Q: What surgery are you having next week?

A: Well, in December 2004, I had a prophylactic mastectomy of the left breast and a touch up to the right side because I had some hardness on that side. I had expanders placed in both sides at that time. Since then I've been having the expanders filled weekly, and next week I will have surgery to remove the expanders and have them replaced by saline breast implants.

Q: Tell me about the recovery from the radiation and the effect it had on you.

A: It was inconvenient to have to get the radiation treatments, which caused me to be late for work each day. I also had burns all across my right chest and armpit. I still have scars from the burns. The radiation also scarred and tightened the skin on my reconstructed breast, so I'm having problems with that.

Q: What problems are you having?

A: My breast tissue is very hard and it is not pliable or stretchy. So when I go to have the expander filled, it is very painful because the skin on my chest will not stretch, so the expander puts a lot of pressure on my ribs.

Q: Will this problem be alleviated with the removal of the expanders next week?

A: No, because the expanders are being replaced by permanent implants. But I believe my plastic surgeon will remove some scar tissue and cut into the scar to help the skin stretch better.

Q: Were there any other effects of the radiation?

A: Just the fatigue.

Q: After the radiation course completed, did you get more or less back to normal in terms of fatigue?

A: In a few weeks, yes.

Q: Now, we talked about the effects and how you felt during the chemotherapy, the mastectomy, and the radiation. Is there any other part of the breast cancer treatment that we haven't talked about?

A: Yes, I am on tamoxifen treatment now.

Q: Now, how does this tamoxifen make you feel?

A: It produces menopause-like symptoms. I have hot flashes during the day and night sweats every night.

Q: Is there anything that the doctors have indicated that they can give you for that?

A: Yes, I am taking a low-dose anti-anxiety medication, which serves a dual purpose. It reduces the hot flashes and night sweats and helps me with some anxiety I was feeling following the completion of the treatments.

Q: Is there any more chemotherapy or radiation planned?

A: No.

Q: You mentioned you are having another surgery next week. Are there any additional procedures planned following that surgery?

A: No, if there are no additional complications, I don't expect to have any more surgeries.

Q: You talked about range of motion in your arm. Have you had physical therapy?

A: Yes, I had one appointment prior to starting radiation. The physical therapist measured my range of motion, then demonstrated some exercises I could continue at home.

Q: Now, let's talk about the prophylactic mastectomy you had on the left breast. Who recommended that?

A: I brought it up to my breast surgeon.

Q: Did she think that was an indicated option?

A: The reason I wanted to discuss it with her was because I had concerns about my original misdiagnosis. I didn't want the same thing to happen if I felt a mass on the other side. She said that I should have a genetic test to see if I had the gene mutation that would make getting breast cancer on the other side more likely. And so I did have the genetic test.

Q: And did you have the gene?

A: I had a mutation on one of my genes, but it was inconclusive – meaning that a mutation is there, but at this time geneticists are not sure if there is an increased possibility of getting cancer from it. There just is not enough research at this time on the mutation I have.

Q: So the genetic testing that you underwent did not give you the information that would indicate that you needed a prophylactic left mastectomy?

A: I don't think it would give that indication for anyone. It is just used as a tool to decide whether you would personally want to have the prophylactic mastectomy.

Q: And how did that inconclusive result lead you to the conclusion that you wanted a prophylactic left mastectomy?

A: It was inconclusive in the fact that they did find a mutation, but don't know what that mutation means. That, along with the circumstances surrounding my misdiagnosis, was enough for me to decide to have the left mastectomy.

Q: When did you speak to your breast surgeon regarding the left prophylactic mastectomy?

A: I believe it was in the fall of 2004.

Q: And when did you have the left mastectomy?

A: On December 15, 2004.

Q: So do you think the time period between fall 2004 and December 15, 2004 was enough time to think long and hard about having this procedure?

A: I thought about it prior to speaking with my breast surgeon. In fact, I recall asking her before my first mastectomy if I should have the left removed at the same time. She had said something along the lines of, "Let's just worry about the right side for now." It was always in my mind that I wanted to have it done. I didn't have to think long and hard about it.

Q: Other than it being in your mind and the inconclusive genetic test, is there any other reason why you proceeded with the left mastectomy?

A: Yes, because of my experience with the delayed diagnosis of the cancer in my right breast. I didn't want to go through that again.

Q: During your recovery period after the left mastectomy, did you have any problems?

A: Just pain and scarring, but nothing unexpected.

Q: So beyond this surgery that you are having next week, you don't have any plans for any further reconstructive surgery?

A: Well, I don't have nipples now, and they can do that but I'm not sure if I will have that done or not.

Q: And you did not have that done at the time of the reconstruction?

A: No, I did not.

Q: Any particular reason?

A: They don't do them at the time of the reconstruction, they wait until you are healed so that they can be placed properly. At this time I don't feel a need for them.

Q: At this time, you are taking tamoxifen and one other drug, correct?

A: Yes, tamoxifen and effexor, the anti-anxiety medication.

Q: And is the plan for tamoxifen to continue for five years?

A: Yes.

Q: And when did the five-year-clock start ticking?

A: In February of 2004.

Q: So you are just a year and a half into a five year program?

A: Yes.

Q: Have you had any recurrence of any cancer anywhere up to this date?

A: No, not that I know of.

At this point, Margaret began asking me about the time I had taken off from work due to the diagnosis and treatment. I had only taken three days off right when I received the diagnosis to attend appointments with regard to the second opinion, then five weeks during the course of chemotherapy, and eight weeks following the right mastectomy and reconstruction. I was then off for four weeks following the left mastectomy, and planned to take ten days off following the expander/implant exchange. Margaret tried to assess the financial implications of the delayed diagnosis with regard to my employment.

Q: Based on what you provided to us in regard to your earnings, have your salary and promotions been affected by the time you had to take off?

A: My annual salary has not been affected, but as far as promotions, I can't say if the perception of my work or my dependability has been changed because of my time off.

Q: All right. Tell me about how this has affected you psychologically and emotionally.

A: Well, it's changed everything. I'm always worried about cancer coming back. And I have a hard time thinking about the future or making future plans because of this fear. I don't think I will ever get over the fear. The relationship with my husband has changed. In some ways it has made us a stronger couple, but this was a lot of added stress in just our first year of marriage. Sexually things are different because I don't have the confidence I used to because of the appearance of my breasts. Psychologically it has all just been difficult to deal with. I'm not sure if you had a specific question or not.

Q: Well, other than how you feel, which I understand, how

has how you feel affected your daily life specifically?

A: In June of 2004 I'd had a couple of panic attacks and I was seeing a psychologist about that. It was around that time that I started on effexor, not only to alleviate the effects of tamoxifen, but also to eliminate the panic attacks.

Q: When you say it affected your relationship with your husband, can you be more specific about that?

A: Yes. It's just that this cancer situation has been the topic of conversation for so long that we just haven't had a normal relationship. All this happened a couple of months after we were married, and I feel like it is not fair that all of the focus has been on me and cancer and not on starting our married life together. That's been stressful for us.

Q: I don't have any other questions at this time.

Without a chance to take a breath, Dr. Kay's lawyer began his questions. They mainly revolved around trying to get at why I never went back to see Dr. Kay after the initial appointment. I couldn't remember why at that time, I thought it was because of a change in my insurance, but later remembered that it was because I had moved out of the area when Joe and I purchased our home. The lawsuit against Dr. Kay and her institution was eventually dropped. She just didn't have as much an opportunity along the way to do the right thing, like Dr. Em did. I still hoped the filing of the lawsuit and learning of my health outcomes would influence how she cared for young patients in her care in the future.

Ten

In February of 2006, two years after I began taking tamoxifen, I stopped taking it so that Joe and I could start trying for a baby (tamoxifen can be harmful to a fetus). I was nervous about discontinuing tamoxifen since it could be keeping any existing cancer cells from growing. I didn't know for sure if the cancer was totally gone – no one can know that for sure. But tamoxifen is still experimental for premenopausal women, so I would never know for sure if it was helping me or not. Because I wanted to get pregnant as quickly as possible to reduce the length of time I would be off the drug, just in case it was helping me in any way reduce the risk of a recurrence, we consulted with a fertility specialist. Both Joe and I were tested to screen for any problems that would prevent us from getting pregnant, and everything was found to be in working order.

Also in February 2006, Dr. Em was deposed. I received a copy of the transcripts a few weeks later. I learned a lot about Dr. Em from his testimony. He was a board certified, tenured professor of obstetrics and gynecology at the teaching institution where he practices. He teaches medical students, residents, and fellows. I also learned that his wife had recently passed away...from breast cancer.

Dr. Em stated in his deposition that there were several times that I had perjured myself in my deposition. He said that I lied when I said that Dr. Kay told me the mass felt like a cyst. He said that while there was a note in my medical record that said I had complained about a breast mass, there was nothing in the record to said Dr. Kay said it was a cyst. Similarly, he said that he never told me that what he had felt was a cyst, or that the discharge was galactorrhea and was normal. He also said that I did not even present with a mass because he clearly noted in the medical record that there was no lump. He said that I lied when I claimed that three doctors, Dr. Kay, Dr. Em and the ultrasound radiologist told me that they thought the mass was a cyst because it was not noted in the medical record. He even went so far as to claim that I had never called to get the ultrasound results because it was not written down in my chart. I believe that at the time of his deposition, he did not remember my visit at all and continued to refer to the incomplete medical records.

At one point, Andrew asked Dr. Em if he would have any knowledge of things that Dr. Kay may have said to me that were not recorded in the medical record. He admitted that he would have no knowledge of any unrecorded conversations, but that no competent physician would tell a patient that there was a cyst or mass in the breast and not document it in the record. Throughout the deposition he holds firm that there was no mass in my breast at the time of his examination. He had written that I was asymptomatic in my medical record, which is why I was not able to get the diagnostic mammogram at that time. I'll never know why he just did not want to believe that there was a mass, let alone cancer, in my breast.

Interestingly, Dr. Em stated that in the first order for a mammogram, he wrote that there was a breast mass and galactorrhea. He said he did this because he was "playing the game," meaning that he did not actually think I had these symptoms, but wrote that on the order so that I would be able to be approved to get the test. Then, a week later on the order for the ultrasound, he noted my case to be asymptomatic. If he would have indicated the breast mass on the ultrasound order, it is possible that the radiologist would have been looking for cancer. Instead they just found "dilated ducts" which Dr. Em admits in the deposition record could be caused by ductal carcinoma in situ.

I couldn't help but laugh when I read Dr. Em's response to one of Andrew's questions:

Andrew: Do you fault Tina for not seeking follow-up treatment between November 2002 and July 2003 (the time following the ultrasound and prior to the visit to the new OB/GYN)?

Dr. Em: I would phrase it this way, Andrew, I'm very surprised that a young woman who is a research associate for a medical association and who holds a master of public health degree would not seek medical attention in the face of a growing breast mass.

I was flabbergasted. He would not admit that I had a breast mass at the time of my appointment, and clearly explained to me at that time that I had nothing to worry about, but is surprised that I would not seek treatment for the same mass? A mass that he states was not even there?

While I was extremely irritated by Dr. Em's deposition, I was glad that the case was making progress.

In March 2006, I was diagnosed with hypothyroidism, and because low thyroid hormone can cause a miscarriage or the child to have a low IQ, our babymaking plans were once again delayed – this time for three months until I could stabilize my thyroid levels. We went at it the natural way, but in September also visited a fertility clinic for intrauterine insemination (IUI), a procedure where our doctor deposited Joe's sperm into my uterus using a thin catheter. We wanted to cover all the bases. While we waited to see if I was pregnant as a result of this procedure, I received a call from Andrew.

"Good news!" Andrew said as I answered his call from my office at work.

"What is it?" I asked.

"Dr. Em's lawyers want to settle the case. They know he is at fault and do not want this case to go to trial. How do you feel about settling the case out of court?"

"I'm fine with it," I said. "I just want him and his institution to realize that what happened was wrong. I'll be happy to put this behind me."

Dr. Em's lawyers offered a sum of money to settle the case that was acceptable to both me and Andrew.

"Let's go with it Andrew. It's time to move on."

And we did. I used the money to buy my one splurge

item – a set of real pearls, a necklace, bracelet, and earrings. The rest was invested for what I hoped to be a very long future. And then it was over. My cancer was in remission and I felt vindicated that Dr. Em and his institution didn't feel confident going to trial over my case, knowing full well that they would lose. My hope was that Dr. Em would be more open-minded to the possibility of cancer with his future young patients. I also hoped this would cause a ripple effect at the institution, causing them to provide physicians there with more education about breast cancer in premenopausal women. I'll never know if this happened, but have faith that everything I went through had some effect.

When I was a kid, I quietly accepted the abuse dished out by my father. I did not take any action against him to stop it, and lived many years with a lot of anger as a result. As strange as it may sound, I was able to let some of that anger go when this case was resolved. Having followed it through to completion, and to have it resolved in my favor, helped me to feel more powerful. I know now the depth of my strength, and know that I will never sit idly by and get taken advantage of ever again.

Eleven

When Joe and I learned that the September IUI was not successful, we were disappointed, but undeterred in our mission. We continued trying at home, and had two more IUIs in October and November.

It was around that time that I was chosen to participate in the Life Beyond Cancer retreat for female cancer survivors held at the world-renowned Miraval Life in Balance spa in Catalina, Arizona, just outside of Tucson. If you've ever been to Miraval, you know what an amazing place this is. Set at the base of the Catalina Mountains in the Sonoran desert, the grounds of the spa transport you to a place of inner peace and reflection. The accomodations are much more luxurious than any hotel I have been to before. It is the vacation spot for celebrities and business tycoons, and I was thrilled to have the opportunity to go for free, since the retreat was sponsored in part by a pharmaceutical company and private contributors.

The purpose of the retreat was to provide workshops, lectures, and group activities that would both prepare participants for a life beyond cancer, and inspire them to start or support existing cancer programs and advocacy efforts at home. I went looking for balance, and for me, at that time, meant a shift of attention from work to self.

While the spa treatments and activities including hikes, horseback rides, and meditative walking through the beautiful cactus-filled desert were experiences I will never forget, the moments of true clarity came to me when I took the time to just be alone, quiet, and still and reflected on my life. I don't often take the time to do this at home, with the normal to-do list of activities always running through my head.

I kicked off my sandles and laid on my back on a stone bench inside the "Kiva," a stone circle enclosing a fire pit. Earlier that morning I sat in that circle along with about one hundred cancer survivors receiving a native American healing prayer. I could still smell the fire. The desert sun warmed my face. A warm breeze passed over me, and I heard a voice whisper, "You are here. You are strong." It was like the those women, my sisters in cancer, and all those lost to cancer, were speaking directly to me. I was ready to put cancer behind me and start my new life.

At the end of the retreat, I had about an hour to spare before I had to leave to catch my flight back to Chicago, so I dragged my luggage to the bird ramada and sat on a bench facing the mountains in this clearing filled with hummingbird feeders. I had never seen a hummingbird in the wild until that day, when at least twenty came to feed mere feet away from where I was sitting. I took this time to reflect on my life and the resolutions I wanted to put into action when I got back home.

- *I am here, I am strong.* I will live in the moment, and

recognize the power of mindfulness and positive thinking.

- I will be a thoughtful giver and a thankful receiver of gifts.
- I will make time for myself to meditate and relax. I will create a perfect space to do so.
- I will make my job something I love to do so it will not feel like work.
- I will do what I set my mind to.
- I will take more risks and chances in life. I will be brave and go for new experiences.
- I will live more and love more, being present and mindful.

It was then, in that bird ramada at the Miraval spa outside of Tucson, Arizona, that I decided to write my story and share it. I had been searching for the reason I had gotten cancer at such a young age, and maybe this was it. I had to bring my story to other young women so that whoever read it would understand the warning signs of breast cancer, and be vigilient in seeking proper care if their doctors do not take their complaints seriously. I had found my mission.

I'm not sure if it happened the natural way or with the help of the IUI, but we found out I was pregnant the day after I got home from Miraval.

My pregnancy was one of the happiest times of my life. I was lucky enough not to experience any morning sickness, food cravings, or excessive weight gain. I did have terrible heartburn, which I believe was caused by the baby being carried so high in my abdomen. The TRAM-flap reconstruction caused my lower abdomen to be pulled tight, which I think pushed the baby higher, placing pressure on my stomach. But the heartburn was nothing in the grand scheme of things.

I resigned from my job in April 2007. I wanted to take the summer off, enjoy the pregnancy, and have lots of time to read, garden, and prepare for the baby. I am grateful that the money we received from the settlement allowed me to have this very special time.

Because of my thyroid imbalance, which can cause a baby to be oversized, my obstetrician planned to induce labor on or before my due date. He called me on a Friday to ask if I was ready to come in the following Monday evening for the induction. While I'd had nine months to prepare for the baby's arrival, one weekend did not seem like enough time. Joe and I were so excited, giggling at the thought of bringing the new member of our family home in just a few days.

After a healthy labor and delivery, Averie Rain Koral was born on August 14, 2007 at 2:10 pm. She weighed a healthy seven pounds and seven ounces, and was 20 ¼ inches long. And despite my fear that chemotherapy had somehow damaged my eggs, Averie was born perfect, with all of her fingers and toes and a bellowing cry that immediately melted our hearts. She was the average baby, to everyone but Joe and I. My sister-in-law, Averie's godmother, was able to experience the birth with us. Needless to say, Averie's arrival was the most amazing experience of our lives.

All of the baby books tell you to be aware of signs of postpartum depression, characterized by unexplainable crying spells. I knew I was susceptible to the baby blues due to my past issues with anxiety, and about three days after bringing her home, it hit me full force. I didn't have unexplainable crying though – I knew exactly why I was crying in the quiet hours of the night while feeding Averie. I was overcome with the fear that the cancer would return and leave her without a mother. For about two weeks, there were times when I would just look at her and not be able to stop crying, realizing that she would never remember me if I died. One night while I fed her, she was looking up at some framed prints I brought home from a trip to Barcelona, Spain. I told her, "You like those pictures? One day I'll take you to Spain." Just then, I thought about cancer coming back and that it was possible that I won't live long enough to take her to Europe. I kept thinking how horrible it would be if my cancer recurred and I knew I would die and have to leave her. I wouldn't be around if she needed me, and someday she would call someone else "Mom." It was rough stuff, and I had a difficult time dealing with it.

Luckily Joe was home for three weeks after she was born and was able to fill in when I needed a break. These dreadful feelings eventually lifted, and while I still fear not being here to witness her life's milestones, I don't think about it nearly as often and can usually block out any negativity and focus on how happy Joe and I are to have her here with us today. It's impossibly sad to think that there is a good possibility you won't be around to help your child grow up, and I know that there are millions of cancer survivors around the world thinking the same thing. Damn cancer.

Some might say that Averie is spoiled. Joe and I spoiled her right from the start by letting her take her first naps in our arms. That baby did not see her bed during the day for her first seven months or so. We just never wanted to put her down. She'd had a hard time soothing herself and getting herself to sleep because we always did it for her. At seven months, we were still walking around with her to get her to fall asleep in our arms before putting her to bed, which is against all the "rules." I know it's because I just don't want to see her cry. I'm sure no parent wants to see their child upset or crying, but I can't help but think that if she only has a limited time with me, I don't want one second of it to be spent unhappy. If that makes me a bad parent, then so be it. It's something that only someone in my position can understand. I also beleive it is impossible to spoil any child with too much attention.

I have no reason to believe that I'm going to die any time soon. I've had CT scans and bone scans annually since my diagnosis, and they have all been clear. While I know cancer can return to complicate my life at any time, I have no reason to believe I have not beat this beast. But it can still be tough at times to shake the experience.

As we inched our way through the Friday afternoon traffic, full of Chicagoans trying to get out of town for the weekend,

I thought, "This is not a good start to this trip." Averie was in the back seat, whining for the last hour and a half. Nothing would appease her. Not her favorite book, animal crackers, or even my singing, which she usually loves. "Just go to sleep!" I pleaded in my mind while trying to stay relaxed and keep Joe from losing it.

We were on our way to St. Joseph, Michigan, a beach town on Lake Michigan, for a weekend getaway. We'd never been to that area before, but based on a recommendation of a friend, and a ranking of the "Best Beach in the Midwest" on a few online travel sites, we were optimistic that this place was special enough to visit. After all, we had a lot to celebrate. This trip was sandwiched between two major events in the Koral family – Averie's first birthday, and my five-year "cancerversary."

I was excited to get away for a few days, hang out on the beach, and just *be* together. We'd celebrated Averie's birthday quietly the day before with cake and a few presents. I was pumped over some aptly-timed research that had been reported in USA Today earlier that week showing that the risk of cancer relapse is low after surviving five years. I knew this was a very general finding, and my cancer was more advanced than many, but I'll take any positive research news that I can get. With a weekend vacation on the horizon, the week could not get any better.

Things took a downturn when, while rushing to get on the road on Friday afternoon, I slipped down the stairs while holding Averie. I went crashing into the baby gate positioned at the bottom of the stairs, and Averie banged her mouth against my head. She was screaming into my shoulder, and when she raised her head, there were blood spots on my shirt. Luckily though, our injuries were minor, no broken bones, no lost teeth. After calming her down, we were off.

Averie finally fell asleep, five minutes before we reached our hotel. She had a bottle and Joe and I put her to bed, and we relaxed a while before going to bed ourselves. As I fell asleep, I hoped a better day would greet us in the morning.

After breakfast the next morning, we gathered all our gear and made our way to the beach. The weather couldn't have been better – sunny and eighty degrees. The sugary sand kept Averie busy all day; she just couldn't get enough of it. After a rough start, the trip was turning out to be all I expected.

I tend to think about cancer not when I'm having a bad day and feeling low, but when I am happy and having lots of fun. I couldn't stop looking at Averie, playing in the sand blissfully oblivious to what was going on in my mind, and thinking about how different things could have turned out for me. It's just so amazing to me that she is here, that *I* am here.

It's been over five years since my diagnosis, and many understand this to mean that a person who has not experienced a recurrence for five years after the initial treatment has no cancer cells or undetected tumors in their body, and that the chance of getting cancer again is the same as anyone else. However, with breast cancer, people are known to have recurrences ten or fifteen years after the initial diagnosis, especially if their original tumor was fueled by estrogen, like mine was. It is difficult to live with the fear that the cancer will come back. What else can I say, other than I hope it doesn't. But if it does, I will fight it harder than I did the first time. I have so much more to fight for now.

My experience with the delayed diagnosis of my cancer has taught me to be much more vigilant when it comes to medical care. I ask questions now, research a lot more, and form better partnerships with my healthcare providers. When Averie was born, she had a heart murmur, which is very common in newborns. We were told that it would go away in a few days if not before we left the hospital with her. A few days later, our pediatrician heard it again, but said not to worry about it. I researched infant heart murmurs, and learned that not all are harmless, but most are. However, hearing the pediatrician acknowledge the murmur and tell us not to worry about it, was all too familiar. I asked to see a pediatric heart specialist who, after further testing, determined that it was indeed a benign murmur. Does that make me an overprotective mom? Probably, but I'd rather be overprotective than have my daughter go through a similar situation as I did.

I'd like to say that the experience taught me to live each day like it was my last, but in my opinion that is just not realistic. I don't spend my days skydiving, traveling around the world, or calling everyone I know to tell them that I love them. Most days are mundane, spent playing with Averie, cooking for my family, gardening or reading. I try to live in the moment as much as I can. If I am playing with Averie, I am playing with her. That's it. Not talking on the phone or watching television as I do it. When she grows up, I want her to remember that I was always willing to spoil her with attention.

My hope is that one day we can live in a world where we can eat clean food, drink clean water, and breathe clean air. My cancer was not hereditary, so I can only deduce that it had an environmental cause. In the meantime, we are trying to live cleaner, and "greener", in an effort to help reduce the chance that Averie or anyone else gets cancer.

Now, over five years and four reconstructive surgeries later, I realize that from the treatments I chose, to the decision to take legal action against my doctors, to the controversial choice to start a family, I did what I felt was right for me. After all, friends and family can bring loads of support, but ultimately you experience cancer alone. *You* lose your hair. *You* are left with the scars. *You* have to be okay with the decisions you make, no matter what the outcome. Luckily for me, my outcome was good health, a loving husband, and a beautiful daughter. I couldn't ask for more.

One of the scariest things about surviving cancer is that I don't know if or when will return. I am basically at the mercy of the universe. The toughest challenge for me, on a day-to-day basis, is suppressing that fear enough to let the happiness of every day life emerge. To stop thinking about dying, and to really experience living. To stop the tears and feel the joy when my daughter smiles, my husband laughs, and my family and friends surround me with comfort and security. I have to go on like this never happened, or else, cancer wins.

Lance Armstrong, hero to cancer survivors everywhere once said, "Birthdays don't really matter much anymore ... for me, I sort of have a new birthday and that's October 2nd, the day I was diagnosed, ... the day we all sort of look to and mark these milestones by one year, two year, five year, ten year. Hopefully, I have a fifty year." My new birthday is August 18. And I hope I have a fifty year too.

Before cancer, Joe and I always used to say, "We're so lucky." We were healthy, in love, had great jobs and wonderful families. We stopped saying it after I got sick. I didn't feel lucky anymore, especially since my odds of getting cancer at such a young age were so small. While watching the summer sun set over Lake Michigan, two days following our daughter's first birthday, and two days before my five year survivor mark, I looked over at Joe, and for the first time in five years, said, "We are *so* lucky."

How to Prevent a Misdiagnosis or Delayed Diagnosis of Breast Cancer

A misdiagnosis or delayed diagnosis of breast cancer can be caused by:

- Failure to order proper tests, such as fine-needle aspirations, mammograms, ultrasounds, MRIs, or biopsies

- Failure to properly read or evaluate test results

- Failure to follow up on test results, such as referrals to a breast specialist

- Failure to order more tests if the results are inconclusive

- Failure to listen to patient's complaints

- Failure to adequately screen for increased risk (age, ethnicity, family or personal history, gender)

- Failure to identify obvious physical findings during examination, such as a breast lump or nipple discharge

There are many steps you can take to avoid or reduce the risk of a misdiagnosis or delayed diagnosis if you suspect breast cancer.

1. See a doctor. Most of the time, doctor's diagnoses are correct and accurate. Don't self-diagnose any breast problem based on the Internet, books, or advice from friends or family. Never avoid

seeing a doctor based on your own suspicions. Provide your doctor with as much information as possible about your symptoms and family history of breast cancer and gynecological cancers.

2. Get a referral for a breast specialist. A breast specialist or surgeon is even less likely to misdiagnose a breast mass than a primary care doctor.

3. Get a second opinion. If you are not satisfied with the care you have received you're your doctor, or if your doctor does not take your complaints seriously, see another doctor. If the doctors agree, the chances of a misdiagnosis are greatly reduced. If they don't agree, be persistent until a correct diagnosis is reached.

4. Ask for a diagnosis. Ask your doctor to specifically name their diagnosis. Exactly what is the diagnosis? Is it a fibrocystic condition? A benign tumor? Breast cancer? Make sure you and your doctor are both clear on what your explicit diagnosis is. Do not let him/her ignore your complaints without giving you a reasonable response as to why you may be feeling the way that you do. If you're not satisfied with your diagnosis, ask for more tests, and question your doctor about what else your symptoms could mean.

5. Ask questions. If you do not understand the diagnosis, and the reasons the doctor has given you the diagnosis, it is difficult to assess its

123

accuracy. Are any other diagnoses possible? What other diseases has your doctor ruled out? Which ones have been tested for or ruled out?

6. Read test reports. Make sure your name is on the report and that the test given was appropriate for your specific condition. If you do not understand the results, ask the doctor to discuss them in further detail with you.

7. Research breast diseases. The best way to feel confident in your diagnosis is to understand the characteristics of the disease. Research your disease, how it is diagnosed, and what tests are typical.

What To Do If You Suspect Malpractice

1. Remain calm. Do not call the doctor accusing a medical mistake. Calmly ask the doctor what happened. Any ethical doctor will discuss your care and why certain decisions were made.

2. If you still suspect malpractice, obtain your complete medical record from your doctor's office.

3. Keep a detailed record of events, dates, conversations, and names of doctors, nurses, and technicians involved in your care.

4. Contact an experienced, qualified medical malpractice attorney in your state. Be aware of the statute of limitations for your state.

Resources for Young Women Facing Breast Cancer

I'm Too Young For This! Cancer Foundation: www.i2y.org
i[2]y is the nation's fastest growing advocacy, support and research organization working exclusively on behalf of survivors and care providers under the age of forty.

Fertile Hope: www.fertilehope.org
Fertile Hope is a national, nonprofit organization dedicated to providiing reproductive information, support, and hope to cancer patients and survivors whose medical treatments present the risk of infertility.

Life Beyond Cancer: www.lifebeyondcancer.org
Life Beyond Cancer is a four-day retreat at the Miraval Life In Balance spa for women cancer survivors and oncology nurses focusing on the many components of advocacy and wellness through and beyond the cancer experience.

LiveStrong Young Adult Alliance: www.livestrong.org
The LiveStrong Young Adult Alliance is a coalition of organizations with the goal to improve the survival rates and quality of life for young adults with cancer between the ages of fifteen and forty. The Alliance is comitted to promoting research and the investigation of the problem, serving as the voice for the issue and promoting effective solutions.

The Young Survival Coalition: www.youngsurvival.org
The YSC is the premier international, nonprofit network of breast cancer survivors and supporters dedicated to the concerns and issues that are unique to young women and breast cancer. Through action, advocacy, and awareness, the YSC seeks to educate the medical, research, breast cancer and legislative communities and to persuade them to address breast cancer in women forty and under. The YSC also serves as a point of contact for young women living with breast cancer.

Made in the USA